Blessings *and* Miracles

Miracles

A Memoir

Miracle Publishing
650 Scranton Road, Suite J
Brunswick, Georgia 31520

ISBN: 978-0-9893682-0-9

Cover Design: Oddball Dsgn

Interior Design: TWA Solutions.com

Printed in the United States of America

Dedicated to my grandmother, Susie Harris.

Without you, I would have never found my passion and never fulfilled my dreams...

Acknowledgments

First, I thank God. If it had not been for You, none of this would be possible. I thank You for strength, wisdom and understanding. I thank You for using and choosing me to be a blessing to others. I give You all the praise and all the glory and I'm here to complete the mission You set for me. I won't ever stop until it's completed. My journey has not been easy, but I understand it all and I'm truly grateful to You.

I would like to thank my wonderful husband, my supporter, and soul mate Alontrake Hill who has been there for me, no matter what, throughout our fourteen years of marriage.

My mother Darlene Jackson who taught and showed me so much. If it wasn't for you and everything that I've been through, I wouldn't be the women I am today. Thank you for encouraging me and helping to make my dreams come true. We did it!

I would like to extend my thanks and love to my amazing and wonderful loving children La'Miracle and Xavier Hill, who encouraged and motivated me not to give up. It's because of the two of you that I pushed myself when I felt I couldn't push any more I want to thank you guys for being my light in my darkness. You're my everything.

My grandmother Susie Harris, my best friend, and now, my "Angel." At a point in my life when I felt so lost, and when there was so much that I didn't understand, you told me that God had a purpose for my life, and you were so right. You showed me that my passion for caring for others in their time of need was important and I so thank you. You will forever be missed, my Angel Susie.

There are so many very special people who have been a major blessing in my life. Thank you all: my father, Jamie Tyre, my brothers David and Jamie Jr. Tyre, stepfather Brian Jackson, Miracle Home Care Inc: Jocelyn Jenkins, Charlene Williams, Sonya Moss, Sherry Reed, Cynthia Keith, Michelle Shay, and Laura McClendon, and the rest of the staff including everyone who's been a part of this wonderful team over the years. Thank you for everything!

I would like to give a special thanks to Victoria Christopher Murray. You took my life and turned it into a wonderful story. I was once told how powerful my story was, but when I read it, the story even inspired me. There's no doubt that what you've helped me to create will inspire others. God has blessed you with a wonderful gift of writing and blessing others. Thank you for helping me.

There are so many in my family and so many friends who have supported me throughout my life. I would never be able to name everyone. But please know that I am so grateful for your love and support over the years, through the good times and the bad. I love and thank you all and I'm so grateful to have you in my life.

Blessings
and
Miracles

A Memoir

Shashicka Tyre-Hill

CHAPTER 1

My earliest memory in life is one that is filled with violence. I was only four years old and we were living in Brunswick, Georgia, which is where I was born. The memory begins as a happy one; I was in the kitchen with my mother, sitting at the table while she stood at the stove, getting dinner ready for me and my two older brothers.

I loved doing that with my mom. I loved watching her cook because sometimes, she would let me help her and I couldn't wait until I would be able to cook on my own. And I loved being in the kitchen with her, especially when she was smiling.

On that day, my mom was smiling. But then her smile went away when my father came into the kitchen.

What I remember most about my father was that I spent a lot of time with him...until he started using drugs. And with the way he came stomping into the kitchen—even though I was only four—I knew there was going to be trouble.

When he started walking toward the refrigerator, my mother looked up at him. "What are you doing?" she asked.

"I'm going to get some of that meat in there."

"What are you gonna do with that meat?"

"I'm gonna sell it."

"No, you're not," my mother said as she jumped in front of him. "You're not going to take that food out of here. That food's for your kids."

My father pushed my mother aside as if he didn't care what she was saying.

"Jaime!" she screamed. "Stop it."

She tried to grab his arm, but he just shoved her away again. Then, she grabbed a knife from the counter.

"Oh, really?" my father screamed. "What you gonna do with that?"

My eyes were so big as I sat there watching them go back and forth, but when my mother picked up that knife, I screamed.

"I'm gonna kill myself," I cried. I didn't know how I was going to do that, but I had to do something to stop my mother and father. I was afraid they were going to hurt each other because they had gotten into fights like this before.

My father was always trying to take things from the house—anything that he could sell so that he could buy drugs. Even though my mother always tried to stop him, my father kept doing it.

But this was worse...now my mother had picked up a knife and she wasn't playing. I was scared that she was gonna kill my father. So I screamed, and I hollered.

"I'm going to kill myself," I kept shouting.

I was hysterical and couldn't stop. Not even when someone started banging on our front door.

"Open up! It's the police!"

My father rushed to the door as my mother tried to calm me down, but she couldn't. I was still crying and now, I think I really did want to kill myself. I may have just been a kid, but I knew enough to know that I really wanted to die.

Two police officers walked into the kitchen and as they looked around, one of them asked, "What's going on?"

"Nothing," my mother said, even though I was still hollering about killing myself.

"Well, something is going on," the other officer said. "Your neighbor called and said that she heard screaming. What's going on with her?" he asked, pointing at me.

"I'm going to kill myself." I told him what I'd been telling my parents. "I just want to die."

It must have been shocking to hear that from such a young child because both of the policemen's eyes got wide. Then, one of them told my mother, "We're going to need to take her to the hospital. She needs to go to Savannah Regional."

"No!" my mother screamed. "She's just a child. She doesn't mean what she's saying. She doesn't even know what she's saying."

But what my parents didn't know was that the police had to take me to Savannah Regional, which was a mental facility. They did that any time anyone threatened to hurt themselves—no matter how old the person was. So that's what happened—the police escorted me and my mother to the hospital.

At the hospital, while the doctors looked me over and calmed me down, the police talked to my mother. She explained what had been going on, how she and my father had been fighting and how I was there in the middle of all of that.

"You and your husband don't need to be together because this is starting to cause problems for your kids," the policeman advised my mother. "Your daughter is here, in a mental facility. That should tell you something."

My parents had been having problems for a long time, but I guess me being at Savannah Regional made my mother really listen and by the time the hospital released me and sent me and mother home, she had made a decision. She told my father that he had to leave.

Things were pretty bad when my mother and father were together. But then when he left, our lives got much, much worse.

CHAPTER 2

When my dad left, he left everything behind, including the bills. It was hard for my mother because she wasn't making much money. As a high school dropout, she never earned more than minimum wage, so she really struggled.

It was hard on her with all of the bills: the rent, the food, the lights and everything else. But no matter what, my mother kept working, even though things never got easier.

Then, six months after my father left, my mother met Gerald.

My mother and Gerald met at Job Core and when she introduced me and my brothers to him, all I could think about was this was a real nice guy. Not only did he help my mother out financially, but whenever he came over, he came with gifts for us. He bought games and toys for us all the time. He took us out to dinner a lot and when we didn't go out, he would sit and watch TV with us.

It was so cool to have him around. With Gerald there, my mother was able to pay the rent and all the other bills without worrying about where the money was coming from. It was a great time. I was happy because she was happy.

I was only about six years old, but I was very aware of everything that was going on around me. One thing I couldn't figure out was how Gerald had so much money. He didn't have a job, but he always had money. My mother had a job, but she never had money.

Of course, as I got older, I realized that Gerald was selling drugs. I guess my mother didn't care about that. As long as he was helping out and it was better for her kids, she was fine with it.

But the good times with Gerald only lasted about a year. I don't know what made him change. I don't know why he became abusive, but the first time he went off on my mother, I knew we were in big trouble.

It happened one day when my mom and Gerald came and picked me and my brothers up from school. When we piled into the car, Gerald and my mother were already fighting. I don't even remember what they were arguing about, but they were both yelling, and the more we drove, the angrier they both got.

As their voices got louder and louder, I became more afraid. I had no idea where Gerald was taking us. He was driving down this long road that I'd never been on before and when I looked both ways, I saw nothing but trees.

Then all of a sudden, Gerald slammed on the brakes, jumped out of the car, ran around the front and by the time he dragged my mother out of the car, my brothers and I were already screaming. He started beating on her with his fists. He just kept hitting and punching her, not stopping. My mother didn't do anything, but try to cover up.

My brothers and I were still in the car, still in the back seat, just watching and crying. My oldest brother, David, had his face pressed up against the car window and the way he screamed made me cry even more. To see my mom getting beat up like that was real hurtful. There was nothing that we could do.

I don't know how long the beating lasted, probably only a few minutes, although it felt like forever. But finally, Gerald got back in the car and then my mother crawled in, too. Neither of them said a word and my mother kept her head down as if she didn't want us to see her face.

It was a long, quiet ride back home.

That was only the first time. From then on, Gerald was extremely abusive and he just never seemed to stop. There were times when I would be asleep and then all of a sudden, I'd hear screams. Right away, I would start crying because I knew what was happening. My mother would rush into our rooms, make us get dressed, then, she'd drag us out of the house. All the time, Gerald would be screaming at her. We would jump in the car and he'd chase us down the road.

Things like that happened all the time. When I tell you it was hell, we went through some things because Gerald's abuse was constant. He would jump on my mother, cut my mother, beat my mother—it was just real crazy.

I don't know why my mother stayed with Gerald. I guess it was because of the way he took care of her when they first started dating. He was so kind and so generous and to my mom, that's who Gerald was. She fell in love with him then, and my mom is the kind of person who loves real strong. And, I'm sure she just kept thinking that one day Gerald would go back to his old self and it would get better.

But it never got better.

Once he moved in with us, the old Gerald was gone. He got real lazy, very comfortable and he put all the responsibility back on my mom. He stopped giving her any money to help out. He stopped helping out in every way. So my mom went back to working hard again. She picked up two jobs, working at the Ramada Inn in housekeeping during the day and somewhere else at night while Gerald just stayed at home. He spent his days in the bed, doing nothing, while my mother worked.

Gerald was out of control, really. He was still selling drugs, but only at night. He didn't stop at selling drugs—now, he was robbing people and he wasn't even ashamed about it. He would have his friends over at our house and they would laugh and talk about the last person they robbed.

He and his friends would hang out at our house during the day, then at night, Gerald would hit the streets. Sometimes, we wouldn't see him for two or three days.

I liked it when he didn't come home because as soon as he came back, he and my mom would start fighting and that meant he was going to beat her.

It happened so much that one time, I was determined to stop it. Gerald was yelling at my mother and I jumped right in the middle of them, thinking that I would block him. He had never hit me, and I figured that I would be able to stop him from hitting my mother.

But he screamed at me. "Get out of the way, Shashicka!"

"No," I said. I was determined to stand my ground.

He warned me again and when I didn't move, he hit me, right in the eye. It shocked me and my mother and it left me with a black eye that kept me out of school for three days.

When the swelling went down, my mother finally let me go back to school, even though the mark was still on my eye. But, my mother had a story ready for me.

"If your teachers ask what happened to your eye, just tell them that you fell off your bike."

At school, I repeated the story my mother told me and satisfied my teachers, but that didn't make things any better at home. Now that I knew that Gerald would hit me, I didn't know what was going to happen next.

That was the only time Gerald hit me, though, his relationship with us was really bad. We never got along with him—it was hard to like someone who was beating on your mother. And he always went out of his way to let us know that he didn't like us. He abused my mother physically, but he abused us mentally.

He would tell us things like, "Your mother and I don't need you," and "We're going to let the Welfare people come and get you."

He would always pick on us and I never understood why a grown man would treat children this way. But as I got older, I figured it out. I would hear Gerald talking about how my mother needed to stop doing so much for us. Well, Gerald wasn't raised by his mother, so I think he was jealous of the way our mom treated us. Even though my mother struggled, she tried her best to do everything that she could for us. Sometimes, she wouldn't eat, just to make sure that we had food. The way she took care of her kids made Gerald jealous. He couldn't stand it and I think sometimes he jumped on her just for that.

That was the way my childhood went—watching my mother get jumped on, beat up...it was just real hard. We struggled just to get by. We struggled having Gerald in our lives.

What was going on at home affected every other part of my life. When I was at school, I was always worried about what was going on at home or what was going to happen when I got there. Was this going to be another night of beatings? There were always questions in my mind about what was going to happen next. So, it was hard for me to focus, it was hard for me to be a good student. It was hard for me to do anything except worry.

CHAPTER 3

The roller coaster that was my life became an everyday occurrence. Day after day. Year after year. Then, one day, when I was twelve, everything changed.

I had just gotten home from school and Gerald was there. I ignored him like I always did and he came into my room, which was something he never did.

He said, "You wanna go get something to eat?"

For a moment, I wondered why he was being so nice to me, but I said, "Okay. Where are we going?"

"Captain D's."

"Okay."

When we got in the car, I was quiet like I always was when I was around Gerald. At first, he didn't say anything to me either, but then after a few minutes, he said, "Shashicka, I need to tell you something."

"What?"

"I need to tell you something about your mom."

I really didn't want to hear anything he had to say, but I didn't tell him that. I just stayed quiet.

He said, "I don't really love your mom."

His words didn't surprise me. I knew he couldn't love her. Not with the way he beat on her. "Why are you with her then?"

He was quiet for a moment. "'Cause I love you."

Now that shocked me. "Me?"

"Uh-huh," he said. "I really love you. You're the reason why I'm with her."

"What are you talking about?"

"Your mom, I don't love her. She just makes me so mad that sometimes all I want to do is leave. But I stay because I always wanted to be with you."

I was so shocked and so uncomfortable, I didn't know what to say. So, I didn't say anything. At Captain D's, I just ordered my food. And when we got back in the car, I stayed quiet, just hoping that he would drive real fast home.

When we got there, I still didn't say a word to Gerald. I just went into the living room and started eating my food.

I thought Gerald was going to go into the bedroom like he always did, but he came into the living room, too. When he sat next to me on the couch, I got up, went in my room, and shut the door.

But he came in right behind me. He stood at the door and said, "All I want to do right now is kiss you. I don't want your mom. I want you."

Was this guy crazy? "Well, that's not gonna happen."

Then, he walked slowly over to my bed where I was sitting and I was shaking, I was so scared. When he rubbed his hand over my hair, I wanted to scream. But, all I did was push his hand away because no one was going to hear me. Nobody else was home. "No, don't touch me. Don't touch me."

But it was as if he wasn't even listening to me. "You're who I want, Shashicka. You're the one."

"No!" I said.

Every second that went by made me even more afraid. What was Gerald going to do next? Was he going to try something with me? And then, I heard the front door open and close.

"Jamie," I yelled out, knowing that it was my brother.

As soon as we heard my brother's footsteps coming toward my bedroom, Gerald backed up, turned around, and rushed out of my room.

Jamie passed Gerald in the hallway and then he came to my bedroom door. "What's up?" he asked.

"Nothing. I just wanted to know if that was you."

I wasn't going to tell my brother because I didn't know what he would do to Gerald. But, I couldn't wait to tell my mother. I stayed in my bedroom just waiting for her. I wasn't worried about Gerald anymore. As long as Jamie was in the house, Gerald wouldn't be coming back to my bedroom.

Two hours later when my mother came home, I hardly waited for her to get in the door. The moment she walked into the house, I said, "Mama, mama, he was trying to sleep with me!"

"What?"

"Gerald!" I said, pointing to him since he was sitting right there in the living room. "He was trying to mess with me."

"What?" my mother said, frowning at me. "What's going on?"

Gerald jumped up from the couch, but I wouldn't even let him talk. I yelled over him as I told my mother the whole story, everything that Gerald had said about how he didn't love her and that he loved me. The whole time I was talking, Gerald was trying to talk over me.

"She's lying on me. She's lying on me," he kept saying.

The more I told my mother, the more upset she was.

When she started crying, Gerald said, "I got to get out of here. She lying on me."

He rushed into their bedroom and my mother followed him.

Gerald kept yelling like I had done something to him. "She just hates me, that's why she's lying," he said.

From the hallway, I could see Gerald start to pull his clothes from the closet and start packing.

"She hates me," he kept saying. "She's trying to get me locked up."

"No, she's not," my mother said. "She's not like that."

"Yes, she is, and I bet you believe her!" he shouted.

"I don't know; I'm just trying to figure this all out."

"There's nothing to figure out," Gerald kept yelling. "She's trying to get me put in jail."

Gerald kept going on and on like this and my mother kept trying to calm him down. But it didn't take Gerald any time—he got out of there. Gerald actually packed up his stuff and left.

I hated that it happened because of me, but I was really glad that he was gone. I did hate Gerald, he was right about that. And, I was glad that he was out of my mother's life. She was the one who was doing all the work anyway and I thought she would be much better off without him.

Life was going to be good again. It was over between Gerald and my mother.

At least, that's what I thought!

CHAPTER 4

With Gerald gone and my mother still working two jobs, I was pretty much hanging out on my own. But, I wasn't just hanging in the streets. I got a fake ID so that I could work and I got a job as a waitress at Shoney's. And when I wasn't working, I spent most of my time with my cousin, Shantelle.

Shantelle was sixteen. She was young herself, but she was three years older than me and most of the time, I would hang out with her at her house.

Shantelle and her mom lived in an apartment complex called The Heritage. It was a bunch of buildings and there were always a whole lot of guys and girls hanging outside. Something was always happening and my cousin knew all of the guys. Shantelle had already had her first child, so she was far more experienced than I was in many ways.

And she was definitely more experienced than I was about sex. She always wanted to talk about it.

"Girl, you're a virgin," Shantelle would say, "you don't need to be a virgin for the rest of your life. You should have sex."

"I don't want to," I told her.

"But, it feels so good. You just don't know."

"I'm scared to do it."

"What are you scared of?"

"I don't know. I'm just not ready for that yet."

Even though I told Shantelle that I didn't want to have sex, she talked to me about it all the time. But then, a year later, I gave in. I had sex not because I wanted to, but because I was kinda pushed into it.

It was with a guy named Lionel, a friend of Shantelle's. He was hanging out with a bunch of guys and Shantelle introduced me to him, but I wasn't all that interested. I wasn't attracted to him at all. He was much older, at least to me. He was eighteen, and already out of school. And, I was only thirteen.

Lionel wasn't doing much for himself. He didn't have a job and I guessed that he was selling drugs or something. But for some reason, Shantelle liked to hang out with him. I think she really wanted to set me up with him, so Lionel was always at her house or we would go over to his place and hang out with him and his friends.

This went on for a couple of weeks and one day, we were at Shantelle's house. As soon as Lionel got there, Shantelle went upstairs with her boyfriend, leaving me alone with Lionel.

We were just sitting there, watching TV and talking about stuff, and then he asked me, "Are you a virgin?"

"Yeah."

"I can't believe you're still a virgin."

I just shrugged my shoulders because his questions were making me nervous. I knew he wanted to have sex with me, but I didn't want to do it.

Right then, Shantelle came down the steps. "Y'all ain't do nothing yet?" she asked. "Y'all should."

I shook my head. "I can't. I'm scared."

"There's nothing to be scared about," Lionel said. "I promise you, I won't touch you, I won't hurt you. You'll be fine."

I wasn't sure how we were going to have sex and he wasn't going to touch me, but Lionel and I ended up going upstairs to one of the bedrooms. We laid on the bed and Lionel kissed me, but I was trembling the whole time.

He really didn't get a chance to touch me. We didn't have sex because I was so scared that I finally just got up. I don't know if Lionel was upset or not. He didn't say anything, we just went back downstairs.

But, I felt bad about that. And two days later when Lionel came over to Shantelle's house, we ended up going right back upstairs and this time, I let him do more than just kiss me. We actually had sex.

I was terrified the whole time. I cried, and I kept telling Lionel to stop, and that it hurt. But eventually, we did it.

I can't say how I really felt about having sex, but one thing did change—I didn't like Lionel all that much before, but once we had sex, I really started liking him. I think I actually fell in love with him.

So after that, we had sex all the time because now, I wanted to be with him. Lionel and I spent a lot of time together. Besides my brothers, he was the first guy that I could talk to. He listened to me and the way he would let me talk, I could tell that he cared about me.

The more we were together, the more I liked him. And the more I liked him, the more sex we had.

It didn't take long...soon, I was pregnant.

I didn't take a pregnancy test or anything. I just thought I was pregnant because I was having the same symptoms that my cousin had told me about when she got pregnant: sore breasts and morning sickness. I had both. But still, I needed to know for sure and only my mother could help me with that.

I know some girls are afraid to tell their mother when things like this happen. But, I wasn't afraid at all. Not only had my mother and I always talked, but I had always been pretty outspoken about everything. So talking to my mother about being pregnant didn't scare me at all.

That night when my mother came home, I told her the moment she came through the door.

"Ma, I think I'm pregnant."

My mother stared at me for a moment as if she didn't understand what I was saying or didn't want to hear it. "What?"

"I think I'm pregnant," I repeated.

"Oh, my God!"

My mother didn't say another word. She just turned around and went into her room. It was only about seven o'clock, but my mother never came back out. She didn't eat dinner, she didn't come out to talk to me, she didn't do anything else. She just went to sleep.

The next morning, I woke up to my mother shaking me in bed. "Come on, I'm going to take you to the clinic."

I got dressed as fast as I could and when I got into the car with my mother, it didn't seem as if she was upset. It just seemed like she was doing a lot of thinking. It seemed like she was surprised. At this point, I guess my mother just wanted to know if I was or if I wasn't pregnant.

At the clinic, the nurse gave me a pregnancy test and they told us that, yes, I was definitely pregnant. I was only fourteen years old and going to have a baby.

On the ride home, my mother still didn't say anything. And when we got back home, everything stayed the same. My mother didn't say a word about it and the next day I went back to school as if nothing had changed.

But then one night, the next week, my mother called me from my bedroom when she came home from work.

"Shicka! Shicka! Come here."

I walked into the living room and then stopped. My mother had bought all kinds of gifts, all kinds of things for my baby: a crib, and all kinds of baby stuff. And now, she was talking like she was very excited.

That made me very happy, but then, I had to tell Lionel that I was pregnant.

We saw each other just about every day, but I hadn't wanted to say anything to him. I didn't want to say a word about being pregnant until I knew for sure.

I don't know what I expected, but when I told him, Lionel was very nonchalant.

"Uh…okay," he said.

And that was pretty much it. He didn't have much to say—at least not with words. He just started coming around less and less.

Of course, it was hard because I really liked Lionel, but my hands were full with my pregnancy. For some reason, I had a lot of complications. From the beginning, I had a lot of bleeding. The first time, it happened, I was really scared. But at the same time, I was a little relieved. I was thinking that I was losing the baby and maybe that was a good thing because I was so young. Maybe I was too young and just not ready to be a mom.

But still, if I was meant to have her, I wanted to take care of myself and my baby. So, I called Shantelle and told her what was going on.

"Girl, we need to get you to the Emergency Room."

She came right over, and we rushed to the hospital. I may have only been fourteen, but I had an ID that said I was eighteen, and since I looked older, I checked myself in.

About an hour later, the doctor examined me and told me that I was probably having a miscarriage.

"There's nothing that I can do for you here," the doctor said. "Just follow up with your physician in the next few days."

He said that as if this was no big deal, as if having a miscarriage happened every day. So, I went home and when I was still bleeding a few days later, I told my mom and she took me to my regular doctor.

Just like the Emergency Room doctor, my doctor said, "I think you're having a miscarriage. Follow up with me in a week."

So, I went home again. When I followed back up a week later, I wasn't bleeding anymore. So everyone—the nurses, the doctor—thought that I'd just lost the baby. But when they did a sonogram, the nurse said, "Well, I see a baby. So, I guess you're all right."

But then the next month, I started bleeding again.

My mother said, "I swear, I ain't never seen anybody with as many problems as you."

She took me to my doctor again and that's when the doctor finally put me on bed rest because he was sure that I was either going to lose the baby or she would come early.

With every complication, my mother was by my side. But she began to doubt that I would ever give birth. "It's going to be a miracle if you have this baby."

I just seemed to have problem after problem, but I guess it was meant to be because finally, the day came when I was really in labor.

I hadn't seen or heard from Lionel for a couple of months, but still, my mother called his house because she wanted him to know that his baby was being born.

But when my mom called, his mother answered the phone and told my mother, "That isn't none of our problem."

So, it was just me and my mom at the hospital and after nine long hours of labor, I gave birth to my daughter. Of course, Lionel wasn't there and he was never there once the baby was born. But that was fine with me. I'd had my baby...LaMiracle, named by my mother because she had kept saying that it would be a miracle if I had this baby. So, when my little girl came out, that's what my mother wanted to name her...Miracle. And, I added the La to put a little jazz to it.

A day later, I took Miracle home with me to my mother's house and when I got there, I called Shantelle.

"I was just calling to thank you."

"Shicka! Aunt Darlene told me you had the baby. A little girl."

"I did. And that's why I have to thank you."

"Thank me? For what?" she asked.

"'Cause I just wanted you to know that if it wasn't for you, I wouldn't have my LaMiracle."

"Awww....is that the baby's name?"

"Yes," I said as I looked down at this tiny infant in my arms. "That's her name and she's a miracle to me. So, thank you, Shantelle. Thank you because without you, I wouldn't have this beautiful baby."

And that is exactly the way I felt. I was grateful for my cousin and I was grateful for my Miracle.

CHAPTER 5

Now that I had my baby, I knew I had to work full time. My mother already had a lot on her financially and I didn't want to add anymore to her. So because of that, I never went back to school.

My mother was concerned about that, but there was no way I was going to go to school while she did all the work. I just promised her that I was going to get my GED.

I got a full time job at Shoney's, where I had actually been working for a couple of years. Like everyone else, the manager didn't know how old I was. The fake ID I had really helped me. I was given the evening shift, and at first, I was concerned about LaMiracle. Who would watch her for me? But it turned out the evening shift was good for me.

The guy that I was dating at the time really helped me out. I took Miracle to Christopher's house and he would keep her while I worked. I wanted a daytime job, though, so that I could be home with Miracle at night. About two months after she was born, I got a daytime job at the hospital, where my mother was working. I worked in the cafeteria.

I'd fallen into a great routine, living at my mother's house with Miracle. The months passed by and as Miracle grew, I became more fascinated and in love with her. My mother felt the same way. She was so supportive of me and she treated Miracle as if she was her child. It was so wonderful to me the way my mother was there, helping me whenever I needed help, teaching me whenever there was something I didn't know. Without my mother, I have no idea what I would've done.

When Miracle was about eleven months old, I decided that I wanted to do something special for my mother.

She had been looking at a vanity set for her bedroom and now that I was working full time, I wanted to buy it for her. When I told her what I was going to do, my mother was excited. But when I told her that I was going to buy it on that day, she wasn't so happy about that.

"You don't have to do it today, Shicka," my mother said. "It's pouring rain out there."

It was storming pretty badly. But, I wasn't going to let a little rain stop me. "I'll be all right. Makeda is going with me," I said, referring to a good friend of mine.

"That's fine, but with all that rain, I would just prefer for you to do it at another time," my mother insisted. "It'll still be at the store tomorrow."

But this was the first time that I was able to do something nice for my mother. And after all that she'd done for me and Miracle, I was just determined. I didn't know why she was concerned with a little rain anyway.

So, when Makeda came over, I bundled up Miracle, carried her to the car, strapped her into her car seat in the back, and then we all headed to the furniture store. Makeda drove so that I could keep my eye on Miracle in the back. In less than an hour from when we left home, we'd made it to the store, bought the set, and arranged for the store to deliver it the next day. I couldn't wait for us to get it. I didn't know who was going to be happier—my mother or me.

When we left the store, I strapped Miracle back into her car seat, then I slid into the front. I was happy, excited...and hungry.

"Let's stop at Popeye's," I told Makeda.

It only took us a couple of minutes to go through the drive-thru and just as I opened the box to start eating my chicken, Miracle started whining.

I turned around and she was reaching for me. "What's wrong, baby?" I asked her.

She held up her arms as if she wanted me to pick her up.

"You want some chicken?" I asked. But when I broke off a piece for her, she shook her head and just kept whining and reaching for me.

"I can't hold you right now," I said to her. "I'll get you out of there when we get home."

But Miracle whined and fussed and cried. She had never acted like this before. She cried so much that when Makeda got to a red light, I turned around, unstrapped Miracle from her seat, and pulled her to the front of the car with me.

"You sure you should be doing that?" Makeda asked. "You should keep her in her car seat. It's safer back there."

"Well you saw her. I don't know why she's so fussy. She's never like this." The moment I had Miracle in my arms, she calmed down. So, I kept her up front with me, making sure that she was steady in my arms. I didn't like having her up front, but my plan was just to hold her for a couple of minutes.

"She'll be all right with me." Looking back up, I saw that we were passing I Street.

"Makeda!" I yelled. "You're missing the turn. You're supposed to turn here!" She swerved the car to the left...and then...the next seconds felt like they moved in slow motion. I saw the other car out of the corner of my eye. I dropped the box of chicken. Screamed. And then, I wrapped Miracle in my arms, right as I felt the impact of the car as it crashed through the door.

I felt the pain, but only for a split second. Because right after that, everything just went straight to black!

CHAPTER 6

The doctors told me that I had been pronounced dead. They told me this once I regained consciousness and started screaming for my baby. But it turned out that even though I had cracked ribs and a head injury that was so severe that my brain had swollen, my daughter didn't have a scratch on her.

"Your baby is fine," the nurses assured me, and then, the police confirmed that when they came to question me about the accident.

"The car was totaled," the police told me. "And the baby's car seat in the back was crushed. But your body was braced around your baby. You saved her."

Just hearing that sent chills through me. I had never taken Miracle out of her car seat before. No matter what, I'd always made sure that she was strapped in because I thought that she would always be safe in her seat.

I thought back to the minutes right before the accident. I'd only taken Miracle out this time because she'd cried and wouldn't stop. Without any words, my daughter told me that she needed me to hold her. I didn't even want to think about what would've happened if I'd just let her cry.

Makeda had been pretty banged up, too, with scratches and bruises and cracked ribs. But I had been the one who'd been critically injured.

The swelling in my brain was the most serious of my injuries. I couldn't be released until the doctors had that under control. It took three weeks for the swelling to slowly go down and the day I walked out of that hospital, I knew that it was nothing but another miracle from God. It was a happy, happy day. I had been pronounced dead, but now I was alive. I knew that meant my life was going to be wonderful. Clearly, I was here because God had a higher purpose for me

And then, Child Protective Services showed up at our house just a few hours after I'd been released from the hospital.

When the lady knocked on our door and introduced herself, I couldn't imagine what she wanted to talk to me about. But after we invited her in and she talked to me and my mother for a little while, she started asking questions about the accident.

"Was your daughter in her child seat?"

"No," I said. "I always have her in her car seat, but this time, I took her out." I went on to explain everything about the chicken and finally pulling Miracle up to the front with me. "My daughter is really living up to her name because if I hadn't had her on my lap, she would've died," I said, expecting the lady to be really impressed.

But she didn't look impressed at all when she said, "Well, you do know that all infants and toddlers are supposed to be in their car seats at all times."

Had she been listening to me? "I told you. She had a seat, but she would be dead right now if I had left her in it."

"I'm sorry," the lady said, sounding as if I'd done something wrong. "But, we're going to have to take this to court. What you did is child endangerment."

How was this child endangerment when I had saved my daughter's life? I couldn't believe this was going to be an issue. Was this lady saying that she would have rather seen my daughter dead? Would that have made me a good mother?

It was weeks and weeks of going back and forth to court, talking to lawyers, sitting in meetings with CPS. There were a few times when I thought they were going to truly take my daughter away from me. Every night I went to bed praying and praying that this would work in our favor.

Eventually, I stood in front of a judge and told my side of the story. I explained that I always had my daughter in her car seat, but this time, I didn't. And when we showed the judge pictures of the car and explained how the police had found my daughter, braced in my arms and shielded by my body, the judge decided to leave Miracle with me.

It was ridiculous to me that I even had to go through that, but at least that was behind me. Miracle and I could go on with our lives without any more fear.

I just didn't know that our lives were going to take a major change in the next few months. And that change came because of my mother.

About six months after the big accident, my mother came into my bedroom with shocking news.

"Shicka, I need to tell you something."

I was sitting on my bed, holding Miracle. "What?" I asked when I looked up at her.

At first, she paused and lowered her eyes like she was having a hard time speaking to me. Then, she said, "I'm getting married."

"Who are you marrying?" I asked, because I didn't know. My mother hadn't been dating, she hadn't been going out at all. So, I didn't know what she was talking about.

That was when she looked up and looked me straight in my eyes. "Gerald."

Gerald? Gerald, the man who had abused her for years? Gerald, the man who had tried to sleep with her daughter? Gerald, the man who was supposed to be gone forever?

It turned out that it wasn't over between my mother and Gerald. Not only had she been talking to him all this time, but she'd even gone to Chicago to see him. And somehow, he'd convinced her that I was lying. He convinced her that he hadn't done anything wrong, that he was just talking to me and I took it the wrong way.

My mother told me all of that, and then said, "So, I'm getting married, and we're going to have a wedding. I want my granddaughter to be in it."

I was already shaking my head before she finished. "I don't think so."

My mother frowned as if she couldn't believe what I was saying. "What do you mean?"

"Miracle is not going to be in your wedding."

"Oh, yes she is," she told me.

"Mama, how can you marry a man who tried to sleep with your daughter? How can you marry a man who said that he didn't want you. How can you do that?"

"You just lying on him," she said angrily.

"I don't have no reason to lie."

"You just don't like him," she said. "You're lying on him because you hate him."

She was repeating all of the things that Gerald had said the day he left. But she was right...of course I hated him. After the way he'd treated my mother over the years, no child could look at the man who beat her mother and not hate him.

So, yes, I hated him, but no, I wasn't lying. I knew the truth, Gerald knew the truth, and I think my mother really knew the truth, too. I think that was why she was so angry. I think that's why she grabbed me and yanked my hair. "You need to stop lying on him!" she screamed.

She hit me a couple of times like she wanted me to fight back.

But, I wasn't going to hit my mother.

Finally, she stepped away from me. She sounded a little out of breath when she said, "If you don't like what's going on in my house, then you need to get your stuff together and leave!"

"Where am I gonna go, Mama?" I asked her. I couldn't believe that she would really put her fifteen-year-old daughter and her granddaughter out on the street.

"I don't care where you go," she screamed. "Just get out of here."

The moment my mother walked out of the room, I began to pack. I wasn't leaving just because my mother told me to leave. I was leaving because I wasn't going to have me and my daughter staying in the same house with Gerald after what he'd tried to do to me.

Even though two years had passed, I could still hear his voice in my head. The way he said, "Oh, I love you. You're the one I want to be with. I've been wanting to be with you for years."

Not only did I still hear those words in my head, but I always thought about how blessed I was that my brother had come home right then because if he hadn't, I truly believe that Gerald would've tried to have sex with me.

So, I had to get out of that house. If my mother wanted me gone, then, I was gonna be gone!

CHAPTER 7

As I packed, all kinds of thoughts went through my mind, especially about money. The money I was making at the hospital wasn't enough for me to get my own place. At least not yet. But that didn't matter. I was still going to get out of my mother's house.

I packed a bag for me and LaMiracle, and then, I walked into the living room. My mother was sitting on the couch, but she didn't get up. All she did was stare at me, as I held my baby in my arms and secured my bag on my shoulder. She didn't say a word, not even when I opened the door, not even when I walked outside. She just sat there and let me leave.

When I hit that street, I had no idea where I was going or what I was going to do. But I was going to have to figure out something quick because I couldn't walk around outside forever. So, I started praying.

"God, what am I going to do. Help me, guide me, show me the way. I can't stay with my mom, you know that. But, I need you to help me 'cause I have to have some place for me and my baby."

I said that prayer a couple of times and then it came to me that I could go stay with my great grandmother, Lottie. She only lived a few blocks away, and as I walked toward her house, I continued my talk with God.

"I really don't understand this, Lord. Why am I going through this?" I asked, thinking about how I'd just been put out of my mother's house. "All I've ever wanted was to be loved. But nobody cares about me. Nobody!" I cried.

Then right there, on that road, I heard God's voice. I'm not kidding. I heard Him talking to me as if He was standing right there.

"Shicka, I'm taking you through this for a reason. I'm taking you through something so that I can bring you to something."

Through something? To something? I was only fifteen, why did God want me to go through something? Those words didn't make any sense to me, but I knew for sure that I was hearing from God. So, I stayed quiet and listened.

"I'm going to take care of you, so don't you worry. I'm going to take care of you and LaMiracle. From this point on, I'm going to always be with you."

I will never be able to explain it so that other people understand, but I felt God's love cover me right there, and I just started crying.

"One day," He said, "you're going to be able to help other people. And anything and everything you ask me for, I'm going to give it to you. It won't be easy, but you will receive it from Me."

With that last word, I was in front of my great grandmother's house. Grandmother Lottie had raised my mother, and even though she wasn't always the nicest person (at least, that's the way she seemed to me) I knew she wouldn't turn me away.

I wiped my tears away before I knocked on her door. When she opened the door, she didn't even ask me any questions at first. She just let me in.

The next day, I told my grandmother what happened and she told me that I needed to go back home with my mother.

"She didn't mean that, Shicka. You need to be at home with your mom where she can take care of you and you can take care of your baby."

But no matter what she said to me, I was never going back there. It was way more than just being mad at my mother. The biggest thing was Gerald. I just couldn't live in a house with him. I wouldn't be able to stand it when he started beating on my mother again. And what about if he tried to sleep with me again? No, I wasn't going to go through any of that.

So, LaMiracle and I stayed with my great grandmother, but not for long. About two weeks later, Grandmother Lottie came to me and said, "You and LaMiracle are going to have to find another place to stay. Either you need to go home and fix it with your mom, or you're going to have to find someplace else because y'all can't stay here."

I couldn't believe it. I was being thrown out again. But my grandmother was in her seventies and I figured having Miracle, who was a toddler, there in her house was too much for her. Plus, I knew the real reason she was saying this—my grandmother thought that if I didn't have any place else to go, I'd have to go home.

But my grandmother just didn't know me because there was nothing in the world that was going to make me go live with Gerald again. I didn't know what I was going to do, but, I started looking for apartments in the newspaper. It only took me a few days to find one that I thought would be great for me and

Miracle: a two-bedroom in the Evergreen Apartments. The only problem was it cost four hundred and fifty dollars.

Without even seeing it, I wanted that apartment, no matter how much it cost. All I had to do was wait 'til payday and get my check. Then, I would go down there and get my own place.

But when Friday came and I got my check, it was only two hundred dollars. Two hundred dollars? What was I going to do with just two hundred dollars? That was less than half of what I needed.

I was so upset. There was no way I was going to be able to find an apartment for just two-hundred dollars and that meant one thing—that I'd have to go home to my mother's house...with Gerald.

I felt like I was in a daze as I left work. I began to just walk, I just wandered down the road. I didn't even know where I was going, but I needed to be by myself to figure this out and get used to the idea of having to go home.

Just the thought of that made me cry. I couldn't do it. I just couldn't. But what else was I going to do? Where was I going to get this money?

I was walking down Stonewall Street when a car pulled up alongside me. A man stopped his car on the side of the road, rolled down his window and yelled out, "What's wrong?"

I have no idea why I started talking to him. I guess it was because I didn't have anyone else to talk to and I was so upset.

"I don't have anywhere to go," I told him.

"What do you mean?"

When he asked that, I began to tell him about all of my problems. I told him everything and then added, "All I have is two hundred dollars and I need four hundred and fifty."

"Well, I can help you," he said.

At first, I frowned. Why was this stranger going to help me?

"I can help you," he repeated. "But you're going to have to give me something."

"I don't have nothing to give nobody."

"Yes, you do."

"Well, what do you want?" I asked him.

"I'll give you the money you need, but you're going to have to sleep with me."

I thought about it, but only for a moment. Then, I opened his car door and jumped right inside. "Okay," I said even though I was shaking.

I was so scared. I didn't know this guy. I didn't know where he was going to take me, I didn't know if he was going to bring me back. I didn't know if he was going to hurt me or even give me the money.

But what I did know was that I was desperate. I needed this money and if there was a chance that I could get it from him, then, I was going to do what I had to do.

As the guy drove, I just kept looking straight ahead, hoping that this was going to turn out all right. In about five minutes, he stopped and I followed him up to an apartment—I guess it was his. I didn't know, I didn't ask any questions.

When he closed the door behind us, I was trembling so hard. I was trembling when he kissed me, I didn't kiss him back. I was trembling when he took off my clothes and laid me on the bed.

And, I was trembling when we had sex.

I couldn't even tell you much about this guy. I never asked him his name, I guess he was about twenty years old, maybe thirty. And, he was all right looking...I guess. I did my best not to look at him.

But what I can tell you was that when we were finished, we both got dressed and he drove me back to my grandmother's house. Right in front of her house, he gave me the money. He gave me all the money that I needed to get my apartment.

I cannot say that I felt good about what I'd done, but I guess that's what happens when you're desperate. My family hadn't given me any choices and I had to have a place for me and my child to stay.

We said goodbye and I never saw that man again.

The next morning, I got up and took the deposit over to the guy who had the apartment. When I got there, he took one look at me and asked, "How old are you?"

"Eighteen," I said, showing him my fake ID. I'd had a fake ID for as long as I could remember. That's how I'd been able to work since I was thirteen.

So, I moved into my apartment, but right away, I knew that I was going to have to get another job. There was no way I would be able to pay rent and buy food, and pay for the lights and all the other bills on what I was earning from the hospital.

I got my job back at Shoney's. And so, there I was, fifteen years old, on my own, and not only taking care of me and Miracle, but my brothers ended up moving in with me, too.

I was glad to have them there. It wasn't a big thing. Since my mother had worked so much when we were growing up, I had taken on that job of being a mother. So even though I was really young, I knew what I was doing.

Having my brothers there was such a blessing. They helped me with Miracle while I worked and that made it a lot easier for me.

That was our household: my brothers, Miracle, and me. And, I took care of all of us.

CHAPTER 8

Darlene Jackson—Shashicka's Mother

It is interesting how two people remember the same story in very different ways. I remember everything that Shicka remembers, though I remember it as a mother. I remember it as a mother who just wanted to do everything to take care of her children.

To really understand everything that happened to my children, you have to understand who I am and what I've been through. And you have to understand generational curses and the fact that history repeats itself whether we want it to or not.

When I was twelve years old, my grandmother, who I called Grandmother Lottie, came and took me away from my mother. My mother's boyfriend was abusing her. She was being beat on and jumped on, and one time, her boyfriend even shot at her in front of us kids. There was a lot going on in that house, but the part that my grandmother couldn't take was that my mother's boyfriend was sexually abusing me.

So my grandmother, who was probably in her early fifties at that time, came and took me to live with her. But not long after that, just two years later, I got pregnant—I was just fourteen years old.

At first, my boyfriend, Jaime, didn't want to have anything to do with me when I told him. And my grandmother, who was elderly, didn't want to be bothered either. So, I was just a kid, pregnant, and alone.

It was a horrible time for me. I was lonely and depressed because I was scared. I didn't have much prenatal care, my grandmother didn't know much about that. And even when I went into labor, all my grandmother did was put me in a taxicab and sent me to the hospital by myself. Can you imagine how I felt? Now, I was really scared. No one had told me what was going to happen or what to expect. I was fourteen, about to have this baby and I didn't know anything.

When the nurse admitted me into the delivery room, she asked me, "Where's your mother, your family?"

"I don't have anyone. No one is going to be here."

"What?" she said. She looked at me as if she really felt sorry for me. "Well, you're not going to be by yourself. I'm going to be with you. I'm getting ready to get off, but when I clock out, I'm not going home. I'm gonna come back and be with you."

And that's what she did. Ms. Mary stayed with me until I had the baby. If it hadn't been for that nurse, I don't know what I would've done.

I gave birth to my son, and took him home to my grandmother's house. But then, my son's father, Jaime started coming around again and he decided we should get married. My grandmother agreed with that. It didn't matter to her that I was so young. She figured since I had the baby, I should get married. So, the following March, that's what Jaime and I did.

Now, I was fifteen and married and I had another son when I was seventeen. By the time I was eighteen, I had my daughter.

Now, I was married with three children. And, I really didn't know what I was doing.

I was so young, and so inexperienced trying to be a wife and mother. There was so much that I didn't know, so much that I didn't understand, even about life, period. I was just a child myself.

So, when my husband, Jaime started using drugs, I didn't even know it. I didn't know the signs. People were telling me that he was on drugs, but what did that mean? And anyway, he was my husband and the one thing I knew was that a wife was supposed to always believe in her husband. I had to stand by him. That's one thing that my grandmother did teach me.

But when so many people kept saying things about Jaime and drugs, I decided to ask him. I told him what other people were saying. But all he said was, "I don't know what you're talking about."

As it turned out, it was all true...my husband *was* on drugs. It took me awhile, but I began to see the signs. First, money was coming up missing from my pocketbook, and then, I found a can that was bent and a friend of mine who was at my house told me, "That's what a person uses when they're smoking crack."

My friend was right. My husband was using crack cocaine.

It was because of crack cocaine that my daughter was almost admitted to a mental facility. The day that Shicka was taken to Savannah General is a day that I will never forget. It was a Friday, and I had just been paid. Since I finally realized that my husband really was on drugs, I gave my money to a girlfriend of mine, a lady who was working with me. I asked her to hold onto my money because I needed to make sure that we had a place to stay and Jaime wasn't even paying the rent anymore.

But when I got home, Jaime was waiting right at the door for me.

"You got your check?" he asked me.

"No."

"Why not? Didn't you get paid? Where's the money?"

"I don't have it," I said as I turned to go into the kitchen.

My husband followed me in there and when he headed toward the refrigerator, I blocked him because I knew what he wanted to do. He was going to try to take our meat and sell it so that he could have drug money.

That's when the fight began and I picked up the knife. All I was trying to do was stop him from taking the food because I had to take care of my kids no matter the cost.

"Stop it, Jaime," I yelled at him. "You can't take this. This is all we got and the kids got to eat."

I don't know if it was the drugs or what, but he didn't care. Jaime and I stood there fighting and that's when Shicka jumped up. She ran to the counter and grabbed a knife.

"I'm gonna kill myself," she screamed as she waved the knife in the air.

I dropped the knife that I was holding and went straight to my daughter. "Shicka, calm down, baby."

But she kept crying and screaming. She kept saying over and over that she was gonna kill herself. There was nothing I could do to get her to calm down and a few minutes later, the police were at our door.

When the officers came in, I tried to explain what had happened. I told them about the drugs and the food and the knife and Shicka. The whole time, I tried to calm my daughter down, but she was still screaming.

One of the officers told my husband that he needed to leave.

"You don't need him in the house with your kids if he's doing drugs," the other policeman explained to me. "You need to let him go."

But even after the officers talked to me and my husband, Shicka was still upset and that's when they told me they had to take her to Savannah Regional since she was still crying about killing herself.

On the ride to the hospital with Shicka, I was just so hurt. I was so hurt that it had all come to this. But it was even worse once I got to the hospital. After talking to Shicka and finally calming her down, the doctors told me that if my husband stayed in our home, they would have to take my children away from me because that environment wasn't good for them.

The choice was easy for me. My choice was my children! I didn't want my husband any more. I wanted my kids. I never wanted them to go through what I'd gone through with my own mother. I didn't want them to be taken away from me. I wanted them to know that I would always be there for them.

Once my husband left, though, that's when the real struggle began. I had never been on my own where I had to take care of everything, where I was responsible for all the bills. I was only twenty one years old with three kids and I felt like life was kinda new to me. Now, I was in charge and I didn't know what to do. How was I going to take care of myself and my kids? I was overwhelmed and confused.

The bills just kept piling up. I didn't make enough money to cover everything and just a couple of months after my husband left, the landlord put a notice on our apartment saying that if I didn't pay the rent, I was going to be put out.

That was when I really panicked.

I needed money, and there was only one place I could go—to my grandmother. But she was even older now. She didn't have any money.

"I don't have anything to give you, Darlene," Grandmother Lottie said. "All I have is my Social Security check."

I left my grandmother's house so upset. Just wandering down the road, I talked to myself, cried, asked God to please help me. What was I going to do if my kids and I got put out? I just kept praying because one thing I did know—the Lord was never going to lead me wrong.

But still, I was scared. Up to this point, I'd always had the kids' father. He always worked and until the drugs got real bad, he always took care of us.

But with Jaime gone and with time running out, I didn't know what I was going to do.

And that's when I met Gerald.

I met Gerald at Job Core, even though I used to see him around town before then. And we just started talking. Gerald was really nice and after a couple of days, I told him what was going on with me because I didn't have anyone else to talk to.

I was shocked when he said, "Don't worry about this, I got you. I'm going to help you."

The first time he told me that, I told him no. "You don't have to do that. I'm praying about it."

"No," he said. "I wanna help you."

Gerald asked me for my address and later that day, he came to my house with the money for my rent. When I looked at that seven hundred dollars, I didn't know what to do. I ain't never had anybody who just wanted to help me like that. Because of him, I wasn't going to be put out of our apartment, and my kids would have some place to sleep.

From that day on, Gerald did everything he could for me. Every day, he came by with something different. One day it was groceries. The next day it would be toys for the kids.

I needed help and Gerald was right there helping me. When there was no one else around, Gerald was there. When there was no one else I could go to or talk to, Gerald was right by my side. And Gerald was a good, good man.

Not too long after that, Gerald moved in and for a long time it was really good. I loved how that man took care of me and my kids. But then after a while, things changed. He became abusive for no reason at all. I had seen a lot of abuse in my life and I figured it was just a generational curse that had followed me. I had seen so much bad, that I almost didn't know what was good. I didn't know what was right and what was wrong.

I kept hoping that Gerald's abuse would eventually stop, that one day he would go back to who he used to be, but it never changed. It just got worse and worse. The beatings continued, but I never left him. I just figured that this was my life. My mother had been through this and she had made it, so maybe this was the way life was supposed to be.

It wasn't all bad with Gerald. When he wasn't being abusive, I really believe that he loved me. Maybe I was making that all up in my head, I don't know. I had always been looking for someone to love me: my mother, my father, my husband. I never felt like anybody really cared about me. So when Gerald came around, that was all I knew.

I never realized that I could have lived a better life. I could have done much better than being with Gerald, but I didn't know that and I was afraid. I had tried it on my own when Jaime left and that didn't work out. Besides that, even if I thought I could make it without Gerald, even if I thought that life would be better without him, how was I supposed to get out? How was I supposed to leave him? Gerald would have never let that happen. He'd already told me what he would do if I tried to leave. He told me what he would do all the time and one time he even showed me.

When I told him that I wasn't going to put up with him beating me anymore, he pulled a gun out of his pocket and pressed it against my head.

"Leave me and I will kill you."

I was so afraid when he said that because I really believed him. I wasn't afraid for myself, though. It was my kids that I was thinking about. If anything happened to me, what would happen to them? I had to be here to take care of my kids.

But once Shicka told me about the things Gerald had said to her, things had to change. At first when Shicka told me that Gerald had tried to sleep with her, I was really confused because I knew my kids didn't like Gerald. Especially Shicka. One thing about my daughter—if she didn't like something, she knew how to step away or get rid of it. So, I didn't know if she was just trying to get rid of Gerald.

But after hearing everything, I told Gerald to leave. Because even though I was confused and I wasn't sure, I wanted to be fair to my daughter. I wanted Shicka to know that I would always be there for her. I would always support her and listen to her.

So, I told Gerald to just get his stuff and go. And he left. I guess he left because he was afraid of what could happen if I called the police.

For two years, I didn't have any contact with Gerald. I just went about living my life, working two and three jobs just to fill up my time. I wasn't involved with anyone, but I wanted to keep it that way. I had been looking for love in all the wrong places and love had done treated me wrong for so long. So, I didn't want to be with anyone except for my children.

Then, Shicka got pregnant.

She was only fourteen, the exact age that I was when I got pregnant. All I could do was remember how I felt when that had happened to me. I remembered how alone I felt, and how scared I was. And, I never wanted Shicka to feel the way that I did. I wanted her to know that I supported her and loved her in spite of her young pregnancy. I wanted to be more understanding to her than anyone ever was to me.

So, Shicka may have thought that I was happy when she got pregnant, but I wasn't. I wasn't happy because I knew it was going to be hard on her and having a baby was going to change her life. But, I loved Shicka and when LaMiracle was born, I loved her, too.

But while Shicka was settling into being a parent, there was something going on in my life.

Gerald!

He had started calling me and the first time he called, he sincerely apologized.

"I'm really sorry, Darlene, for how I treated you. I hope you can forgive me."

At first, I didn't believe him. But then every time he called, he said the same things. Over and over again. At the time, I wasn't in a relationship with anybody because I was afraid of making the same mistakes that I'd made with Jaime and Gerald. There were no Steve Harvey relationship books out at that time. There was nothing and no one to help me, direct me and guide me to what was right. So since I didn't want to bring anyone else into my kids' life, I had stayed by myself.

But the more Gerald called, the more I started to listen. And after a while, I began to think that my kids were growing up. Shicka had had her baby, my sons were older, too. Maybe it was time for me to start thinking about me because I was really tired of being alone.

Of course, no matter what decision I made, I would always be there for my children. Whenever they needed me, if they ever needed me, I was going to be there. But, I began to think that maybe *my* life would be better if I let Gerald back in.

"I really have changed," he told me. "And, to prove it to you, I want us to get married. I want to give you a big wedding."

He had never talked about getting married before and the more I listened to him, the more I believed him. I began to think that maybe Gerald and I could be together again. Maybe love had finally found its way to me.

I decided that not only was Gerald and I going to get back together, but I was going to marry him. Agreeing to do that made me really happy. I figured that by being married, everything would change. Gerald would change, the kids would change and it would all be fine. I really wanted to give Gerald a second chance.

I wanted all of my children to celebrate at the wedding with me because I just wanted to be happy for once in my life. And what would make me happy was having everyone who I loved around me when I said, "I do."

But when I told Shicka, she wasn't happy all all. All she kept saying to me was, "I'm not gonna be there."

Her words really hurt because she is my only girl and more than anything I wanted her and LaMiracle there with me. I tried to talk to her, but she wouldn't listen to me. All she wanted to do was argue.

"I want you there," I told her. "I really want you and Miracle there."

"Well, we're not going to be there 'cause you don't need to marry him."

I couldn't remember a time when I'd seen my daughter so upset. She just kept telling me no over and over. She was talking back to me, something that she'd never done before and I finally had to say something to stop her.

"You know what, Shicka. Two grown people can't stay in the same house."

I was only talking about the way she was talking back to me, so when Shicka started packing up her stuff, I was shocked. I never told her to get out. I never wanted her and Miracle to leave.

But she wouldn't listen, she just packed up everything. Before she walked out the door, she told me, "As long as you stay with Gerald, I'm never coming back. You're gonna marry him, but you're gonna regret it. Because he don't love you, and I do."

I couldn't see it then, but in the end, Shicka was right. I did regret marrying Gerald. He didn't love me.

But the thing is, mothers are not perfect. Mothers make mistakes, too. I made my share of mistakes, but one thing is for sure. All I ever wanted to do was love my kids and take care of them.

I just did the best I could.

CHAPTER 9

It was official, I was fifteen and I was on my own.

It wasn't easy. Really, it was hard, but it was something that I had to do since I wanted to be on my own. But it was tough because with me and my brothers in that apartment, everything cost more. Besides the rent, the light bill was higher, I had to buy food for all of us. There were so many expenses.

But even though financially it was a lot, my brothers being with me was a good thing. They kept me company and they were always there to help me with my daughter, especially in the summer when they weren't in school. My oldest brother, David, went back and forth between me and my mom's. I guess that was his way of checking on our mother, especially now that Gerald was back. But my other brother, Jamie, was always there with me and because of him, I didn't have to pay for child care for LaMiracle. So, Jamie became Miracle's primary caregiver while I worked.

I had the same routine every day. I would work and come home, work and come home. All I was doing was working to take care of my daughter and help out my brothers.

Every day before I left for my second late-shift job, I checked to make sure that Miracle had everything she needed. One day, I saw that we didn't have any milk and Miracle was low on diapers, too. Since it was only two-thirty and I didn't have to be at my job until four, I decided to run to the store myself rather than have Jamie do it later.

So, I rushed into Jamie's bedroom to tell him. LaMiracle was lying next to him in the bed and both of them were asleep. I shook my brother's shoulder. "Jamie, I'm getting ready to go to the store. I've gotta get a few things for Miracle before I go to work."

He didn't open his eyes, he just mumbled, "Okay."

Then, I checked to make sure Miracle was still asleep because since she had started walking, every time she heard that door open, she was ready to go. She wasn't even two yet, just about nineteen months. But my daughter always wanted to go somewhere.

She was sleeping soundly, just like Jamie, so I went back downstairs, grabbed my purse, and ran out to my car.

I couldn't have been gone for more than twenty minutes since I only had to pick up two things. But when I pulled into my parking space at the apartment complex, the first thing I saw was Jamie. He was outside, rushing around, turning his head from side to side, as if he was searching for something.

I frowned and jumped out of the car. "Jamie!" I called him. "What's wrong?"

He rushed over to me. "Do you have Miracle?"

Right away, my heart started pounding. "No! I left her in the bed with you. What's wrong?"

"I can't find her. I thought she was with you."

I shouted out my daughter's name. "Miracle! Miracle!" Now, I was the one running around looking everywhere for my daughter. I was frantic as I kept calling her name and rushing from one end of the complex to the other.

When I walked down my hallway, my neighbor who was across the hall from me, opened his door. "You're looking for your daughter?"

"Yes," I said, hoping he knew something.

He said, "Well, the police took her."

"The police? What do you mean?" I said, not feeling any relief at all. Why would the police have my daughter?

"The police took her," he said again, and then he shrugged as if that was all he knew.

"Jamie!" I yelled out to my brother.

When he came running down the hall, I told him what our neighbor had told me. We both ran into our apartment and my hands were shaking as I called the police. While the phone rang, I didn't even know who I should ask for. All kinds of questions were in my head: why did the police have my daughter? How did they get in my house and why did they take her? How did they get in without waking up Jaime?

Thank God it only took one phone call to find Miracle. Just as my neighbor said, the police had my daughter. I told them that I would be right there.

As I stepped out into the hallway, my neighbor asked, "Did you find her?"

"Yeah. The police have her, but I don't understand any of this."

"Well," he said, lowering his voice, "I didn't want to tell you before 'cause I didn't really want to get involved, but the lady next door to you called the police."

"What?"

He nodded. "She told the police that she heard Miracle crying and when she peeked through the window, she only saw Miracle. So, she opened up your door and took your daughter and then called the police."

He didn't even have to tell me who he was talking about. I didn't know the lady's name but ever since I had moved into those apartments, she had been real nosey. She was always in my business, asking questions, watching me and my brothers as we left and came back to the apartment. I think she suspected that I wasn't really eighteen and she was trying to figure out what I was doing on my own.

I was so upset that she would do this, but I couldn't think about my neighbor now. I had to get Miracle. I drove down to the police station so fast, I was thankful that I didn't get a speeding ticket. I rushed into the station and spoke to one of the officers at the front desk. I told him who I was and he nodded.

"Yeah, we have your daughter. She's in the back room," he said, pointing behind him. "But, she'll be out in a minute. We're just checking her out."

"Checking her out, is everything okay?"

"Yeah," he nodded as if I didn't have anything to worry about. "Just have a seat over there."

For the first time since Miracle was missing, I felt better. At least I was in the same building as my daughter and I would be able to take her home in a little while. I took a deep breath, took a seat, and thanked God.

As I sat there waiting, a woman dressed in a suit walked by me. She nodded, and said, "Hello," but I didn't pay too much attention to her since all of my attention was on that back room where the policeman told me that Miracle was.

But I did notice that the woman just walked past all the policemen and headed straight to the back.

About five minutes later, the woman came out from the back, only this time, she wasn't alone. She had Miracle in her arms.

I jumped up. "Thank God," I said, anxious to hold her myself. I reached out my hands, but the woman twisted so that I couldn't get to Miracle and she pushed me away.

I frowned. Who in the hell was she and why was she taking my daughter? "Give me my baby!" I yelled. "Give me my baby."

"I can't do that."

"What do you mean? That's my child."

"No," she said, swiping at me again like she was trying to keep me away from Miracle.

Then, she moved toward the door. I yanked her hair, trying to stop her. I wasn't going to let her go anywhere with my child. But the moment I grabbed that lady, five officers rushed out from behind the counter.

"Stop it," they yelled.

And before I could do anything, they started beating me with their sticks.

I screamed as I let go of her hair and covered my face with my arms. What was going on? Why were they beating me when this woman was the one who was trying to kidnap my child?

I fell to the ground and two officers held me down while another one twisted my arms behind me and put the handcuffs on.

"What are you doing? I'm trying to get my baby," I yelled.

One of the officers helped me to my feet. "She's with Child Protective Services," he said, as he directed me to sit in the chair. And then, he explained. "CPS is taking her because your daughter was in the house by herself."

"No she wasn't," I shouted. "My brother was in there with her."

"Well, the witness said that she didn't see any adult or anybody in there at all and that means she has to be taken into custody."

"Into custody? What does that mean?" I cried. Were these people really going to take my baby away from me?

"That means she'll be placed in foster care and you're going to have to go to court to get her back."

Now, I really cried, but Miracle being taken away was only one of my problems.

"Now, we have to place you under arrest," one of the policemen said as I watched that woman walk out the door with my daughter.

"What? For what? I told you. My brother was in the apartment. My baby wasn't by herself."

"Not for that. For assault. You attacked the social worker."

"I was just trying to get my daughter," I cried.

But none of them were trying to hear that. They read me my rights, then asked me a couple of questions—one of them being how old was I?

I had been so used to using fake IDs and lying about my age: to get a job, to get an apartment. But this time, I told the truth. Because I knew the difference between being sixteen (which I was) and eighteen (which my ID said I was.)

Because I was sixteen, the police took me to Waycross, the youth development center for youth offenders. If I had been seventeen, I would have gone to the jail with adults. But the way I was feeling right then, it didn't matter. All I cared about was LaMiracle. What was going to happen to her?

CHAPTER 10

O n the entire forty-five minute ride over to Waycross, I didn't think about myself at all. All I could think about was my daughter. Where was she? What was she doing? She wasn't even two years old, so she didn't know what was going on and I knew that she would miss me. I just prayed that she wasn't scared.

The moment the police car stopped and they took me inside the building, I asked if I could call my mother.

"She doesn't know where I am," I told them. "I have to tell her."

A policewoman led me to a desk with a phone, and as I dialed my mother's number, I felt tears coming to my eyes. I tried not to cry when I got her on the phone and told her what happened.

"Oh, my God," my mother said. "They took my baby!"

My mother wasn't talking about me. She was talking about LaMiracle. I knew that she loved me, but she loved my daughter like she was her own.

"Where is my baby?" my mother cried.

"Mama," I said, trying to calm her down. "Mama, please."

"Okay, okay." I could tell my mother was trying to take a couple of deep breaths, but she was still upset when she said, "We have to do something."

"I know, Mama. I think we're going to need to get a lawyer."

"Okay, okay. I'll get right on it. We'll find Miracle and we'll get you out of there, too. Let me see who I can call, I'll get the money."

So many thoughts were coming out of my mother's head, but once she said she would get the money, I knew she would go to my Uncle Bull. Bull wasn't really my uncle, he was my mother's godbrother, but he and my mother were so close, he had always been like an uncle to me. My Uncle Bull was heavy into drugs and he was the only one who had enough money to get a lawyer. But if he had money for a lawyer, I didn't want one for me.

I told my mother, "Don't worry about me. Just get my baby. That's my main concern, Mama. I just want you to get Miracle."

"Okay," my mother told me. "We'll get Miracle."

When I hung up the phone, I was relieved, but I wouldn't feel totally okay until my daughter was safe with my mother.

After my call, the guard escorted me into the main part of the building where I got signed in.

"How long am I going to be here?" I asked.

"You'll be here until your court date."

As the officer led me to my room, I couldn't believe what had happened. I was in a juvenile detention center and I hadn't even done anything wrong. All I'd done was go to the store. Then, at the police station, all I was doing was trying to get my daughter. If that lady from Child Protective Services had explained who she was, I wouldn't be in this trouble. I'd be out, working on getting Miracle home.

But now, I felt helpless.

"Here we go," the female officer said as she unlocked a door to one of the rooms.

I stepped inside and then, the officer closed the door behind me without saying anything else.

My eyes roamed around the stark white room that was about half the size of my bedroom at home. Most of the room was taken up by bunk beds, a sink, and an aluminum-silver toilet. And the room was so bright it almost glowed with the fluorescent lights.

Instantly all of that white, all of that bright light gave me a headache.

I don't know how long I stood there silently, in front of the door before the girl that was in there jumped down from the top bunk.

She asked, "What's your name?"

"Shicka," I told her.

"My name is Shameka. Hey, that kind of rhymes."

From that point forward, Shameka and I were friends, especially after I found out that she was from Brunswick, too. She told me all about Waycross, how we would be spending most of our time in our room since they only gave us an hour a day to go out with the other girls.

"How many other girls are in here?" I asked her.

She shrugged. "I think there are about fifty or sixty."

I sat down on the bottom bunk, which had a mattress that was so thin, I could feel the bed rails underneath it. When I laid down that night, it wasn't only the cheap mattress that kept me awake, it was all the white around me and the bright lights above. I don't know why, but they never turned out the lights at Waycross.

I hardly closed my eyes that first night, nor the next night. And both mornings, I woke up with a headache from the glowing white and from not knowing anything about my daughter. In between the nights, I spent most of my time in the room. Like Shameka told me, we were let out of our rooms for just an hour every day to socialize with the other girls. All the other time, we were back in our room, just talking to each other.

Shameka and I talked about all kinds of things, like how we were going to get our lives together and what we were going to do once we were let out of that place. Shameka had several charges against her including theft and a child charge like me. When we weren't talking, we prayed together for ourselves and for our children.

Two days later, I was able to speak to my mother again and she filled me in on what had happened since I'd been locked up.

"Your uncle is taking care of things," she said. Just like I'd thought, Uncle Bull was going to handle this. "He got an attorney for Miracle."

"Good," I said even more relieved. Once Miracle was with my mother, I would be able to stop worrying completely.

"And, he's working on getting a lawyer for you," she said. "The attorney said that he thinks he can get you and Miracle's court date at the same time so both of you will be home next week."

That gave me a lot of hope and made the next days in Waycross a bit easier, even though the nights were still hard. Every single day I woke up with a headache.

Just like my mother said, the next week, one of the guards came to the door and told me that my court date was in the morning.

"That means you'll probably be going home," Shameka told me.

"You think so?"

She nodded. "It depends on the judge, but since that's your only charge and you've never been in trouble before, you'll probably be going home." Shameka almost sounded like an expert.

That night, I tried to go to sleep, but it was hard thinking about how in the morning, I would get to see Miracle again. I just prayed that the judge would listen to me and know that I would never do anything to hurt my baby.

I just prayed that in the morning, the judge would let me be Miracle's mother again.

CHAPTER 11

The next morning when I got to court and I took one look at my baby, I had to hold myself back from running over to Miracle and grabbing her from that same woman's arms. The lady holding Miracle was the same lady from Child Protective Services who'd taken my baby from me in the first place. But if God had heard my prayer, Miracle and I would be going home together.

When the court session began, both attorneys got down to business explaining the situation and what had happened.

First, the State called their witnesses. The only person to testify for them was my neighbor—the nosey lady who called the police on me in the first place.

As she sat on that stand, I just stared at her. I couldn't believe that I was here and going through all of this because of her. But like I said, she'd always been nosey. And her nosiness got me in trouble.

The attorney asked her why she called the police.

"Well, I heard a little baby screaming and hollering and when I opened my door, the screams got louder. I could tell that the screams were coming from the apartment next door and I knew a young girl lived in there. So, I peeked in the window and saw that little girl crying by the door."

"What did you do next?" the attorney asked.

"I kept knocking on the door and ringing the doorbell. But no one answered. I was so afraid for that little baby. So then, I tested the door to see if it was open and it was. I was so afraid for her, so I just took her with me so that she would be safe."

The whole time she was talking, I was shaking my head because she was lying. First of all, I knew Miracle wasn't screaming and hollering. She may have been whining because she'd heard the door open and she wanted to go with me, but that's all she was doing.

I believe that lady just opened up the door, grabbed my daughter, and then called the police.

Next, my attorney called my brother to the stand.

"I was in the apartment with Miracle," Jamie explained. "She was sleeping right next to me and when I rolled over and she wasn't there, I got up and started looking for her."

"Did you hear anyone knocking on the door?"

"No, sir."

"Did you hear anyone ringing the bell?"

"No, sir. I didn't hear none of that. I don't think she rang the bell or knocked on the door 'cause if she did, I would've heard it."

After that, the attorney put me on the stand and I answered a few questions about where I lived and worked and what happened that day.

The judge nodded the whole time and then when I got down from the stand, both attorneys spoke for a little while—I guess that was their closing arguments.

When the attorneys finished, the judge was quiet for about a minute before he finally spoke.

"The first thing I want to do is commend you, young lady," he said, looking down at me. Then, he looked at everyone else in the court. "Because I want to let all of you know that I actually went to her apartment. When I heard how old she was, that really shocked me that a sixteen-year-old girl could live on her own that way." He looked at me again. "I'm really amazed by you. I want to let you know that you've done a great job. Your apartment was clean and well-kept. When I walked in there, I would've thought that I was walking into a grown person's home."

He went on to say, "I even spoke to the apartment manager and asked him why did he lease you that apartment. He told me about your ID." He paused. "Your fake ID." The judge chuckled a little bit. "You're awfully bright to be so young. So, let me ask you, why are you living by yourself?"

I glanced over at my mother who was sitting next to Gerald. All this time that they'd been married, I hadn't gone over there when Gerald was home, so I hadn't seen him.

"Well, since I had my daughter and I didn't want to put it all on my mother, I thought I should get my own place," I lied. "I knew that I could take care of myself. My mother always had to work so hard, so a lot of times I had to help my mother out by taking care of me and my brothers."

The judge nodded. "Well, did you know that your mom wants custody of your daughter?" Before I could answer, he asked, "What do you think about that?"

I looked over at my mother again, and then, I looked at Miracle sleeping in the arms of the lady who was with CPS. There were so many thoughts running through my head. Of course, I wanted Miracle to be with my mom rather than in foster care. But then, I thought about Gerald and what he'd done to me. I was really scared about what he could do to LaMiracle if she was there.

I guess because I didn't answer right away, the judge spoke up. He said, "I'm going to tell you what I recommend. I recommend that your daughter goes home with your mom because frankly, that's where you need to be. You need to go home with your mother, too. So, if I give your daughter to your mom, will you promise me that you'll go back home with your mother?"

I nodded, even though in my head that was not what I wanted to do.

I guess the judge could tell that I wasn't really happy about that decision, but I would do anything I had to do to be with Miracle.

Then, the judge looked over at my mom. "I'm kinda struggling with this decision," he said to her. "Honestly, I don't want to give Miracle to you, but I know that's what Shashicka would want and this allows Shashicka to be with her daughter." Then, the judge glanced down at some papers before he started speaking again. "I want you to know that I've read over your husband's history." He was talking to my mother, but he started talking about Gerald. "This guy has been in trouble before and if it wasn't for your daughter, I wouldn't give you custody. But since Shashicka is going to be there and since she's already shown just how responsible *she* is and how determined she is to take care of her child, this is what I'm going to do." Looking back at me, he said, "So, Shashicka, you and Miracle can go home...with your mom...today."

I wanted to run over and grab my daughter right then, but I could tell that the judge wasn't finished and I didn't want to get into any more trouble.

"One last thing, Shashicka," the judge said. "You have to vacate the apartment that you had immediately because first of all, you're too young to be on your own. The deal is that you go with your mother, understood?"

I nodded again, and this time, I spoke up. "Understood," I said.

When he hit that gavel against the top of his bench, I jumped up and ran to Miracle. The lady actually smiled as she handed my daughter to me and I hugged Miracle as if I hadn't seen her in a year because it certainly felt that way.

I walked out of the court with my mother, my daughter, and Gerald. We all rode to my mother's house, but as soon as we got there, I put Miracle down to sleep and then went over to my great grandmother's house.

I had to talk to somebody because what the judge had said and what he had decided was heavy on my heart.

My Grandmother Lottie hugged me tight when she opened her door. "It is so good to see you," she said. "I was so worried about you and LaMiracle."

"Thanks, but I need to talk to you," I told her.

She led me to the couch and once we were sitting down, I told her everything that had happened in court. At the end, I said, "But Grandmother, I'm not going to do it. I'm not going to do what the judge said. I'm not going to live with my mom and I don't want my baby there either."

My grandmother nodded as if she understood, but then she said, "Shicka, let me tell you this. If the judge gave your mother custody, your mom is not going to let nobody mess with your baby. Your mom loves LaMiracle as if she gave birth to her herself. She's not going to let anything happen to that baby. What you need to do is look at this as an opportunity. An opportunity for you to get on your feet so that you can do what you need to do. So just go home with your mother and take care of your baby."

I understood what my grandmother was trying to say. She was right. LaMiracle would be safe with my mother. Gerald wouldn't try anything with her since she was just a baby. But as for me, I couldn't go back there—I couldn't go to my mother's house. Not with Gerald there.

"Okay," I said. "But, can I stay here, just for a couple of days?"

"Yeah, Shicka, but just remember that you have to go back to your mom's. That's what the judge ordered."

I nodded like I agreed with my grandmother, but I didn't. I had no idea how I was going to do it, but I was going to find a way to once again be on my own.

All I had to do was figure something out—just like I always did.

CHAPTER 12

That night at my grandmother's house, I really slept for the first time in almost two weeks. I was so glad to be able to turn off the lights. I was so glad that the room wasn't small. I was so glad that the walls weren't bright white.

The next morning, I woke up without a headache and I was starting to feel better already. The only thing—I didn't know what I was going to do.

That day, I just hung around my grandmother's house, and all day long, she kept telling me that I needed to go home. I pretended like I was listening to her; I wasn't. Then, the next day, my Uncle Bull called and asked me to go out to lunch with him. He took me to Eddie's Soul Food Restaurant and the first thing I did when we got to the restaurant was thank him for what he had done for me.

"I really appreciate it, Uncle Bull. I know you spent a lot of money to help me and LaMiracle and I am truly grateful. I will never forget this."

He nodded. "No problem, but it did cost me quite a bit of money. I'm going to need you to pay me back."

"Okay," I said. "I'll be going back to work in a couple of days and as soon as I get my paycheck, I'll give you what I can and I'll keep giving you money until it's all paid back." Plus, I was thinking about the settlement I was going to be getting from the insurance company from my car accident. My mother had sued her insurance company and I was supposed to get twenty thousand dollars and Miracle was going to get five thousand dollars.

But when I told my uncle that, he shook his head.

I frowned. "Well, what do you want me to do?"

"I need you to get a place. An apartment. And then, just allow me and my brother to come to your place whenever we need to. All I'll want is a key to come in and out when I need to."

"That's it?"

"That's it," he said. "I'll even give you the money you need for the deposit and the rent and I'll help out with the rent all the time if you need me to."

"Really?" This was beginning to sound better and better.

He nodded. "I'll help you get the lights on and everything else. You won't have to worry about anything for the first month. Then after that, you can take over whatever bills you can."

"Okay," I said, thinking this was not only a really good deal, this was exactly what I needed. This was perfect timing since my grandmother wasn't going to let me stay with her for too much longer. She really wanted me to go home to my mom's. With my uncle's help, I could get that apartment since I still had a fake ID.

As soon as I got back to my grandmother's house, I got the newspaper and started looking for a place and right away I found a two-bedroom, one bath duplex that sounded pretty good. I called the guy, and arranged to meet with him the next day. After I spoke with him, I called my uncle back to tell him how much the apartment was going to be.

The next day, Bull came and gave me the money before I met with the guy who owned the apartment. The duplex was really kind of out-of-the-way. It was in an alley, off to itself, and if you didn't know that the apartment was there, you would definitely miss it.

So, I filled out the application, gave him the deposit and rent money, he gave me the keys and I called Bull.

"Great!" he said when I told him I had the keys. "So you ready to do this?"

"Yeah," I said. "I wish I could stay there tonight."

"Oh, you can. We'll go get your things from the other apartment since you have to move out of there anyway, and anything else you need, I'll get it for you."

So Bull and some of his friends went with me to my other apartment and those guys moved everything out of my old place into my new one in just a couple of hours.

I couldn't believe how lucky I was to have this happening and happening so quickly. It was really a blessing. Now that I had a place, once I started working again, I could get situated and get Miracle back with me. Even though I wanted her, she had to stay with my mom. I wasn't going to do anything to risk the courts coming in and trying to take her. So, I left her there.

I wasn't as worried about her being there with Gerald as I had been before. My grandmother helped me to see that my daughter was safe with my mother. As much as my mother loved LaMiracle, she wasn't going to let anything happen to her.

So, I went about just living my life, working, and trying to save money for when Miracle could come and live with me. I had been in the apartment for just a couple of days when my uncle called me.

"Shicka, now you remember you owe me, right? You remember that I paid for your lawyer for you and Miracle, right?"

"Yeah," I said. Of course I remembered. I had already told my uncle that I would never forget.

"Okay," he said. "So, I need to use your apartment tonight. Can you go get a hotel and I'll pay for it?"

"Okay," I said because like he said, I owed him. Not only did I owe him for what he had done for me and Miracle, but I owed him for even having an apartment.

As I packed an overnight bag, I wondered what Bull wanted with the apartment. It was probably for women. He and his friends were probably going to have some kind of party with a lot of women. That had to be the reason why he wanted me out of there.

So that night, I stayed at a hotel, then went home the next day. Every week or so, my uncle would call me, remind me that I owed him because of what he'd done for me, and then ask me to get a hotel room. I got used to it and didn't really think it was anything more than him throwing a lot of parties.

But one day, when Bull asked me to get a hotel room, I didn't take my overnight bag with me. I went to work and planned to go back to my apartment after work to pick my bag up.

When I got there, Bull was sitting around the kitchen table with some other guys.

"I'm just coming to pick up my bag," I said.

"Okay, sure," Bull said kind of quickly, then he glanced at the other guys.

I looked over at the men and frowned. On the table were these bricks that looked like they were made of white powder.

There had to be six or seven blocks of that white stuff. I had no idea what it was, so I just went back into my bedroom, got my bag, and then I left.

About two weeks after that, Bull called me again.

"Now, Shicka, remember that you owe me, right? Remember what I did for you and Miracle?"

I had no idea why he always said that and as much as he said it, it was starting to get on my nerves. Not that I wasn't grateful; I was. I just didn't need to be reminded of it every day.

He said, "I need you to do me a favor, Shicka."

"Sure," I said. "You want me to get a hotel?"

"No, I need to know when are you off?"

"Off from work?"

"Yeah."

"Well, I'm not off until the weekend."

"Perfect. Then, I need you to go to Miami. I need you to go drop some money off and pick up a bag."

"Well, okay," I said, slowly with all kinds of questions in my mind. The request was kind of strange, but I knew my Uncle Bull would never put me in any harm or danger or anything like that. So whatever he wanted me to do, I could do it.

"Great. And one more thing—you have to go by yourself. You can't go with anyone else. You have to go alone."

Now, it was beginning to sound even stranger, but like I said, he was my uncle. So, I wasn't worried about what he was asking me to do. No matter what, he would always keep me safe.

"Okay," I said again. "But that's kinda far. I ain't never been out of town. Plus, I don't even know how to get to Miami."

"You don't have to worry about that. We'll come over on Friday and give you everything you need. I'll give you the directions, the money, everything."

"Okay."

"And, you'll have to leave at like three o'clock in the morning so that you'll get there by eight."

I started feeling a bit uncomfortable now, but I didn't want to tell him no, specially because of what he'd done for LaMiracle. If it wasn't for him, she'd probably still be in foster care.

So on Friday, like he promised, my uncle came over, gave me the directions and a bag full of money. "You're going to be going to this hotel," he said, handing me a piece of paper. "You should get there by eight and the room is already in your name. Then at eleven, a guy named Money is going to come over and he's going to give you a bag and then you give him the bag with the money."

His name is Money? That sounded funny to me, but I kept that to myself.

So, I followed my uncle's instructions, got in the car at three in the morning and on the whole ride down to Miami, I was scared. I had never taken a trip before, let alone a trip like this by myself. It was dark and so scary. The glare of the car lights zooming toward me in the opposite lane were blinding.

I kept thinking that something was going to happen. I was going to get a flat tire, I was going to get in an accident. I was going to mess up in some kind of way and disappoint my uncle.

I'm not sure how I did it, but I finally made it to Miami in one piece. When I got to the hotel, all I could do was flop onto the bed and turn on the TV. I couldn't wait for eleven o'clock to come so that I could head back home.

At eleven sharp, someone knocked on the door. I opened it up, and the guy that my uncle told me about walked in, looked around as if he wanted to make sure that I was alone. Then, he said, "You Shicka?"

"Yeah."

He handed me a duffle bag, but then, he said, "I need you to meet me at one o'clock." He gave me a piece of paper with another address. "It's a hotel and the directions are on that paper. Bring that," he pointed to the bag he gave me, "and the money with you." Then, he left.

When I looked in the bag he left, there was nothing but clothes in there. I knew my uncle hadn't sent me all the way to Miami for some clothes, so I waited until one, then drove over to where Money told me. It was hard to find, but I finally found it. The hotel was small and in the back of an alley.

Money was in a car with two other guys and when I pulled up next to him, he jumped out. "Give me the bag that I gave you earlier," he said.

I handed him the bag from where I had it on the front seat, then, he got back into his car. I watched as he and the other two guys started stuffing something inside the bag. I frowned, and leaned over a little, trying to see what they were doing. But, I couldn't see anything and I couldn't figure out what was going on.

A minute later, he got out of the car again. "Open your trunk," he told me.

He put a bag in the trunk of my car, I gave him the bag with the money, and then he left.

It wasn't until I started to drive back to Brunswick that I began to really feel suspicious. I started wondering what was in that bag that was in the trunk? I was thinking that I should've looked inside because now, this was not feeling right. I didn't want to get caught up in anything wrong or illegal.

On the whole ride back, I prayed to God that these guys didn't have me involved in something. But on the other side of my head, I kept thinking that this was Uncle Bull. He wouldn't do anything that would get me into trouble. He wouldn't do nothing like that.

In five hours, I was back home and my uncle was waiting right there for me at the duplex. He took the bag out of the trunk before I got a chance to check to see what was inside.

"Thanks, Shicka," and then my uncle was gone.

I was glad that was over. But then about two weeks later, I received the same telephone call.

"Shicka, when are you off?"

"Next week, I'll be off on Wednesday and Thursday."

"Okay, great. I need you to do the same thing for me."

This time, I just didn't want to do it. No matter what my uncle had done for me, I wasn't feeling right about this.

"I really don't want to do it, Uncle Bull. It was a really long drive," I said, not wanting to tell him the real reason was because I thought he was doing something shady. "I didn't get much rest along the way."

"Oh, you owe us. Do you know that I spent twelve hundred dollars to get the lawyer for you and another twenty-five hundred for LaMiracle? If it wasn't for me, you would've still been in Waycross and your daughter would've been in a foster home."

"Okay," I said, giving in. I

So the next Wednesday, I ended up doing the same thing— driving to Miami, meeting the guy in the hotel. But this time, when Money was getting ready to put the bag in the trunk, I said, "No, sir. First, can I see what's in the bag?"

He hesitated, but then he said, "Look, I'm just gonna tell you 'cause you seem like a real nice person, but what you're doing for Bull is serious."

"What do you mean?"

"Well, I just want you to know that you need to be careful because you're transporting."

"Transporting?" I said, not having any idea what he meant.

He nodded. "You're transporting about five kilos. So, you need to be careful because if the police stop you, you could go to prison for a very long time."

I don't know why, but I was shocked. I guessed I was really naive. I mean, once I thought about it later, what other reason would my uncle have for sending me with a bag of money to meet some strange guy?

Money had to feel really comfortable with me for him to even tell me, 'cause I knew that drug dealers didn't talk about these things. He gave me some more instructions.

"Just focus on getting back home. Don't have no telephone contact with nobody, be very careful about where you stop on the road and what you do because if people knew what you had, they'd kill you. This is all illegal and it's all dangerous."

At least now, I knew what I was doing, but knowing made it much worse. Because now, I was scared. On the whole way back home, I couldn't do nothing but pray.

All the way home, I kept saying the same prayer over and over. "Please God, don't let me get stopped. Please God, I didn't know what I was doing. Please God, please protect me."

God had to be with me because just like the last time, I was home in five hours and my uncle was there at the duplex waiting for me.

But this time, I jumped out of the car, so upset. "Listen," I said to my uncle, "I didn't know what y'all had me doing and I'm not gonna ever do that again because I'm never going to jeopardize my freedom. If you cared anything about me, how could you let me do this? How could you put me in this position?"

My uncle looked at me as if I wasn't making any sense. "You didn't know what we were doing? How do you think we came up with that money?" he asked. "The money that you needed for court didn't fall out of the trees." He went on and on about how he had helped me, but finally, he broke down and told me everything that they had been doing—how they were using the duplex to cook up the drugs and how they kept the 'keys' in the attic.

The whole time that my uncle was finally being honest with me, I kept thinking how much danger he had put me in. Somebody could've came into the apartment, and with me being there by myself, somebody could've killed me.

"If you don't want to do it anymore, you don't have to," my uncle said. "But we're going to need you to stay in a hotel while we clean things up here, okay?"

"All right." I gave him the bag and then drove to the hotel where I always stayed. I just hoped that my uncle would get out of that house quick!

CHAPTER 13

When I got to the hotel, all I could do was sit on my bed and think about everything—what the guy in Miami had told me, what my uncle had told me. Wow! What had I been doing? I had been so blessed that nothing had ever happened to me.

I didn't want to just stay in the hotel room, so I called my girlfriend, Tyisha, to come over so that we could hang out. I really wanted to do something so that I could get my mind off of all of this drug stuff that my uncle had me involved in.

"What do you want to do?" Tyisha asked me when she met me at the hotel.

"I don't know. I just want to get out of here. I just want to do something."

So, we got in my car and I just started driving with no idea where I was going. Tyisha and I were just talking, when she said, "Wait, Shicka, did you see that? Somebody's calling us back there."

"What?"

"Two guys were flagging us down back there."

Just because I didn't have anything better to do, I turned the car around and rolled up into the parking lot of In and Out. I parked next to a car where one of the guys who had flagged us down was standing. The other guy was sitting in the car.

"What's up?" I said.

The one who was outside came closer to my car. "Nothing. We just wanted to get a closer look at you two beautiful ladies."

Tyisha and I smiled.

I said, "Y'all live around here?"

He nodded. "What about you?"

"Yeah," I said.

He said, "My name is Lamar."

Tyisha and I told him our names, but he was the one doing all the talking. His friend wasn't saying a word. So, I looked over at him and said, "Hey, I know you."

"How you know me?" he said, finally speaking up. "You don't know me."

"Yeah, I do," I said.

He got out of the car and walked over. "Well, if you know me, then what's my name?"

"I don't know that," I said.

We laughed.

He said, "Well, my name is Tre."

So, the guys stood outside of the car, talking to us for a while, asking what we were up to.

Then, Tre said, "Y'all wanna go get something to eat?"

"Okay," I said. "I'll drive."

The guys hopped in the car and Tre sat in the front with me. We went to Abraham's, then sat around and talked like we were already good friends. After we finished eating, Tre and I exchanged numbers before I took the guys back to their car and then, I took Tyisha home.

The next day, I left the hotel and went back to the duplex, but I knew I needed to find a new place to stay because I wasn't trying to be involved in all of that stuff my uncle was doing. I wasn't trying to be involved in no drugs. Plus now, I was really afraid to stay in that apartment by myself.

That's why I asked Tyisha to move in with me. When she said she would, I went and picked her up that night.

But even though I had someone there with me, it wasn't enough. I still wanted to get out of there. I needed to find a new place to stay and I was hoping that by the time I did that, I'd be able to get Miracle back, too.

A couple of days after we met those guys, Tre called me.

"Hey, Shicka. What's up?"

"Nothing. What's up with you?"

"Well, I was just calling 'cause I want to come see you."

"Okay."

"So, what's your address?"

I paused for a moment and all kinds of things went through my mind. Why did Tre want to see me? Why did he want my address? Why did he want to come to my apartment? My uncle had always told me not to tell anyone where I stayed and finally, I knew why. If anyone knew that I lived in a drug house, I could be in danger.

I couldn't tell Tre where I really lived, so I gave him a fake address 'cause now I knew that I really needed to be careful.

"Okay," Tre said. "I'll see you in a couple of hours."

Of course, Tre never got to me since I didn't give him my real address. But a week later, I went to hang out in the mall and couldn't believe it when I bumped into Tre.

"Hey, how you doing?" I asked him, wondering what he was going to say. After I gave him that fake address, I never expected to see him again.

"Don't think I don't know that you gave me a wrong address. That was dirty."

"What's dirty?"

"Sending me over to those people's house."

"What people?"

Then Tre went on to tell me how he went to the address that I'd given him and he knocked on the door, waiting for me. And then through the window, he saw an old white man coming to the door. "Man, when I saw them, I hauled ass and got out of there!"

I couldn't help it, I started laughing.

"I apologize," I said. "It's just that we had just met and I didn't know you, you know?"

"Yeah, alright," he said, though I could tell that he was still kinda pissed.

We started talking about what had been going on, but after a few minutes, he said that he had to get going.

"Okay. Are you gonna call me?" I asked him.

"No. If you want to talk to me, then you're gonna have to call me this time. You still have my number, right?"

"Yeah."

"Okay, then if you give me a call, I'll give you another chance."

I laughed. "I'm going to call you," I told him.

"We'll see."

That night, I did call Tre and after we talked for a little while, he didn't seem so mad anymore. After we'd been on the phone for a while, I told him that I wanted to put some rims on my car. "So, can you ride with me to Jacksonville 'cause I know of a good place down there to get them?"

"When you going to Jacksonville?"

"Probably tomorrow," I said. I had gotten a call from my lawyer and the settlement check from the accident was ready for me to pick up. So, one of the first things I wanted to do was get those rims for my car.

"Well, I don't know too much about Jacksonville," he said. 'I can tell you how to get there, but you just go 'head. I don't think I want to take the ride 'cause I have some stuff to take care of here."

"Okay," I said. "I'll call you tomorrow."

The next morning, I went to the attorney's office early, and then after I got my check, I called Tre for the directions to Jacksonville. When I came back, I wanted to get something to eat, so I stopped at a McDonald's and I could not believe it when I ran into Tre again!

"What are you doing here?" I asked him.

"The same thing that you're doing. I'm getting something to eat."

He laughed and then he jumped into my car with me.

"So, where you going?" he asked.

"I'm just riding around."

"Yeah, I saw the rims. They're looking good."

"Thank you," I said.

And then we started talking again. Just like we did at the restaurant and just like we did at the mall. It seemed like it was always so easy to talk to Tre. He was so interesting and so cool. I really liked being around him.

"Well, I gotta get going," Tre said after a while. "I can't just sit in this car and talk to you all night, can I?"

I laughed. "No. But, I'll call you."

After that, Tre and I talked all the time and hung out together a lot, though I made sure that we never hung out at my house.

I wasn't interested in dating Tre or anything. I wasn't interested in him like that. Like I said, he was just cool and I liked being around him.

One night, after hanging out with my girlfriends, I called Tre to see what he was up to.

"I'm at the Waffle House," he said. "Meet me here."

So, I went over there and picked him up. When Tre got in the car, I could tell he'd been drinking or something. He seemed like he was a bit intoxicated.

I never did any drinking and I never did any drugs. After what I saw with my father and the way he behaved, I was afraid of what drinking and drugs could do to you.

I hadn't ever seen Tre drunk before. "What's going on?" I asked him.

"Can I spend the night with you?"

"Okay," I said. "That's cool." The only reason I agreed is that I figured I knew Tre well enough now that I could let him come over. He wasn't one of the bad guys that my uncle was always warning me about.

So, I took him to the duplex and the moment I opened the door, Tre stumbled inside and fell right asleep on the bed.

The next morning, he woke up, looking around and frowning. "Where I'm at?"

"My house," I said.

"How did I get here?"

"You don't remember?"

He shook his head. I told him what had happened, then took him back to the Waffle House so that he could get his car.

Tre and I kept talking like we had been doing, and so a few weeks later, when he asked if he could come to my house again, I didn't worry. I said yes.

This time, though, it was different. Tre didn't just fall asleep. This time, we had sex. And once we slept together, Tre never left. He never went back home. He just moved in.

Tre got there in August, and in December, I found out that I was pregnant.

CHAPTER 14

I couldn't believe it. I was pregnant! This was not what I wanted to happen. First of all, I hardly knew Tre. I had just met him four months before and didn't like him like that. We were just good friends. And, I didn't want a baby.

"I already have my daughter," I told Tre. "And I don't even have custody of her. I'm trying to get my life situated, so I don't want any more babies right now."

"Shicka, I want you to have my baby," he said.

"But, I can't right now."

I could see that Tre was really hurt by my decision, but he said, "Well, you know what I want. But if you don't want to do it, I can't stop you. It's your body, it's your life."

I nodded. "I really want to get an abortion."

"How much does it cost?"

"Four hundred and fifty dollars."

"Okay, I'll give you the money." Then, he walked out of the room.

But as the days passed, and I watched Tre and thought about it some more, having an abortion was not what I wanted to do. Really, it wasn't something that I *could* do. I just couldn't kill my baby.

So, I told Tre my decision. "I changed my mind," I said. "I'm going to have the baby."

Tre grinned like he was so happy. He was feeling it, but I wasn't because like I said, I wasn't into him like that. I just knew that having the baby was the right thing to do.

Tre was really happy with my decision and about a month later, he asked me to marry him.

"I don't know about that," I said. I wasn't trying to hurt his feelings, but how was I going to marry somebody that I really didn't know? And that's what I told him.

"We don't really know each other," I said.

"We know each other enough to have a baby."

"Yeah, but we have to do that. We don't have to get married."

"Okay," he said. "Okay for now."

And it was okay. I was happy with the way things were with me and Tre. He was great to have around, especially since I was still at the duplex. So, I felt safer with him there. And whatever I needed, Tre made sure that I had. Things were perfect as I tried to get myself situated, tried to get ready to have this baby, and tried to get in the position to get Miracle back.

But then one day while Tre was out, I got a call from my uncle and right away, I could tell that he was not happy about something.

"What's going on over there, Shicka? What's going on at the apartment?"

"Nothing. What do you mean?"

"Well, I heard you were dating this guy and you got him over there, living with you."

My uncle went on and on about how Tre was no good for me and how he was going to end up hurting me.

I knew what this call was about. My uncle didn't even know Tre, so this had to be because he was afraid that I was going to tell somebody his business. But he didn't have anything to worry about. I wasn't going to say a word, especially since I could get into just as much trouble as he could.

"I really like him," I told my uncle. "And, I really feel comfortable around him, too."

"Well, I'll tell you what, then. I'm going to come over there and get what we got to get and then you and him can figure out how you're going to pay for that place."

"Okay," I said. But even before he hung up, I wondered what was going to happen. My uncle was paying most of the bills, which was the only reason why it had been so good staying in that place.

Just like he said, that afternoon, my Uncle Bull and two of his friends came right over to the duplex, took all the drugs out of the attic, all the paraphernalia, all the scales and pots and everything they had hidden with their drug business.

Before my uncle walked out the door, he dropped his key on the kitchen table. "Now, you all are going to have to pay for this place. We're gone!"

The moment he walked out the door, I wondered what in the world was I going to do? I decided that I needed to tell Tre everything because I was going to need his help.

That night when he came home, I sat Tre down

"I have something to tell you," I said.

"What?" He frowned. "This sounds serious."

"It is." And then, I told him everything: how my uncle had helped me, then asked for my help. I told him about the apartment, the trips to Miami, what I had found out, and how my uncle had called and came for his stuff today.

"So, now, we're going to have to pay for this apartment because my uncle isn't going to do it anymore and I don't know how we're really going to be able to do it."

Tre had sat there quietly the whole time and just listened. When I finished, he said, "Shicka, they were just using you. They shouldn't have involved you in all of that. I know, 'cause I never brought my drugs around you."

"What?" I asked confused.

That was when Tre told me what he was involved in. I couldn't believe it. Once again, someone in my life was hustling and I didn't know anything about it. Yes, I was young, but having seen it enough times, by now, I should've figured it out.

But the thing was, Tre never brought that stuff around me, so I guess it really wasn't my fault that I didn't know.

"I didn't want you involved in that," Tre said. "But this is how I make my money."

All I was thinking was *here I go again.*

"You don't have to worry," he said. "I won't ever bring that stuff around you."

And, Tre kept his word. If he hadn't told me, I would've never known that he was a drug dealer. But dealing with drugs wasn't the only surprise he had for me. A few weeks after my uncle came and got his stuff, Tre and I went out to dinner and in the parking lot of the restaurant, he asked me to marry him...again.

"Shicka," he said, as he pulled a ring out of his pocket. "I really want us to do this. I really want to marry you."

As I looked down at the ring I had so many thoughts: I was carrying his baby in my stomach, I didn't want to have another child and not be married, I didn't want to be judged by everyone else, and I wanted to do everything that I could for my baby.

So because of all of that, I said, "Yeah, I'll marry you."

Even though I said yes, I knew I wasn't getting married for the right reasons. But, I was going to do it anyway because Tre was good for me and good to me. He cared about me and would take care of me and our baby. That was why I agreed to marry him.

We didn't set a date or anything. Neither one of us was in a big hurry to make it official. But we continued to live together. And the more time we spent together, the closer we became. We just kept getting closer, and closer and closer.

CHAPTER 15

Two months after Tre asked me to marry him, I got a phone call.

Tre and I had just walked into our house. I was coming home from work and Tre always came to my job to follow me home, just to make sure that I got home safely. That's just the kind of guy he was—he really cared about me.

The moment I walked inside our door, though, my cell phone rang.

"Hello," I answered.

"Hey, how you doing? This is Tasha."

Tasha was a girl I'd met through Tre. During the day while I worked, Tre hung out with his friend, Darrel and Tasha, who was Darrel's neighbor, hung out with them sometimes. I'd met Tasha a couple of times when I'd gone with Tre over to Darrel's house.

"Yeah, what's going on?" I asked her. "Something wrong?" I couldn't imagine why she was calling me. It wasn't like we were friends or anything.

"No, I just wanted to let you know that me and Tre are sleeping together."

I turned around slowly and looked at Tre. "What?"

"Yeah, I want to let you know that we're sleeping together and he calls me all the time, we hang out together and everything."

While Tasha kept talking, I just kept staring at Tre.

I didn't say anything and Tasha said, "What? You don't believe me? Well remember that time when you came over here looking for him at Darrel's house? He was right next door, at my place, in my bed. "

"What?" I said again.

"If you come over here, I can show you and prove it to you."

I was still holding the phone to my ear when I said to Tre. "You and Tasha are sleeping together?"

"What?" he yelled. "What you talking about?"

I hung up the phone without saying goodbye to Tasha. "Are you sleeping with her?"

"I don't know what you're talking about," was all he kept saying. He kept marching around the apartment calling her crazy, calling her a liar. It was like he wasn't even listening to me.

I wasn't getting anywhere with him, so I said, "You know what? We're both about to go over there to find out what's going on because you ain't gonna be staying here with me and messing with someone else. And I'm pregnant with your child? It's not gonna happen! I'm gonna go over there and find out what's going on."

"We don't need to go over there. I can tell you what's going on—she's lying."

"If she's lying then when we get there, you can prove it."

"You don't need to go over there," he said as if he could talk me out of it.

But that wasn't going to work. I was going to go and face Tasha. "I'm going over there and if you want to be with me, you need to get in that car, too," I said. I wanted to see what Tre was going to say about this when he was standing in front of Tasha.

I was pissed and Tre knew it. So, when I jumped in his car, he did, too. Tre drove, but on the whole ride over, he kept saying he didn't know what Tasha was talking about and why she was saying all of that.

But I wasn't trying to hear any of that. I wanted to see what Tre was going to say when he was standing in front of Tasha.

The moment we pulled up to where Darrel and Tasha lived, I called Tasha back and told her we were outside. She came right out, stood by the car, folded her arms and told me, "Everything I said was true. Tre and I are sleeping together. We've been messing around for a while now."

I let her have her say, then turned to Tre.

"Is this true?"

Tre was so upset. He looked at Tasha and called her all kinds of names, whores and everything else. Tasha and Tre went at it and it seemed like they were never going to stop. So, I just turned away. I wasn't going to be a part of this mess.

I started walking down the block, shaking my head the whole time. I couldn't believe that I had gotten myself in this position.

Tre jumped in the car and started following me, driving slowly as I stomped down the road. "Shicka, listen to me," he yelled out the window.

"No. I don't want nothing to do with you!"

"Just listen to me," he begged.

"Just go and be with her 'cause I don't have time for this. I'll raise my baby by myself. I'm just done."

This went on for a couple of minutes and a couple of blocks before Tre said, "Okay, but at least let me give you a ride back to the apartment. I don't want you walking. You're pregnant and I don't want nothin' to happen to the baby."

That made me stop and think. Tre was right. I needed a way back; it was definitely too far to walk. And just because I was mad at him, I didn't want to hurt my baby. So, I went to the car and when I got in, I said, "Just don't say nothing to me." I kept my eyes straight ahead. I didn't even want to look at Tre.

"All right," he agreed.

He kept his word and stayed silent, though I could tell that he was dying to talk to me. The moment he stopped the car in front of our house, I got out and ran to the door. I tried to slam it right behind me, but Tre was there, blocking it so the door wouldn't close.

"Shicka, just let me talk to you for a minute. Let me explain."

I didn't want to let Tre in. I didn't want to hear him say anything because there was nothing he could say. There was nothing that was going to take the pain away. I was just so hurt by it all. So hurt by what Tasha told me. I had never felt hurt like this before, a pain that went all the way down to my heart.

But then, I wondered why did I feel this way? All this time, I'd been telling myself that I didn't really care for Tre. If I really didn't love him, then why was I so hurt?

I guess my feelings for him were deeper than I wanted to admit.

Finally, I gave up because I was just too tired and I let him in the door. He sat on the couch and I sat in a chair across from him.

"Look, Shicka, I'm gonna tell you the truth. Me and Tasha were messing around because I wasn't sure about us. And you have to admit, you weren't sure about us either, right?"

I didn't answer him at all.

"You kept telling me that you weren't sure, right?" he asked. When I didn't answer him, he kept on. "But I know that I love you and you're the one I want to be with."

Still, I stayed quiet.

"Shicka, I really do care about you. I really, really do."

This time, I answered him, but not with words. Tears started falling from my eyes because I could tell that he meant what he said. I could see that Tre really did care about me. And from the past, I knew that there wasn't anything that he wouldn't do for me. Anything that I wanted, Tre always got for me. It didn't matter what he had to do. It didn't matter how much it cost.

But even with that, I didn't know what to do. I didn't want to be with him if he was going to be messing around with other girls. But on the other hand, I really did care about him, too. Now, I knew that for sure.

I still didn't say anything. I just turned to go into the bedroom and he followed me. I was still crying, but finally, I did have something to say.

"You said you wanted to marry me," I said as I laid down in the bed.

"Yeah, I do."

"Well first, there are a couple of things that you're going to have to give up."

"Like what?"

"Well, Tasha for one."

"Of course," he said. "I don't want her. That's a given."

"And...selling drugs."

Tre paused for a moment and then nodded. "Okay," he said. "But, I'm only giving that up because I want you to really know that I want to be with you. I love you."

"Okay, then." I paused because I wanted to see what his reaction was going to be to what I had to say next. "So in the morning, we're going to the courthouse to find out what we need to do to get married."

"Okay," he said, without missing a beat. "I don't have a problem with that."

"Okay," I said.

I figured that getting married was the answer to this problem. Because if Tre was one to mess around, then he would never mess around once we got married. People took their vows seriously, no one would want to mess with God that way—at least that's what I thought. Marriage changed most people and marriage would change Tre.

So, the next morning, just like I said, we got up and went down to the courthouse. But when we got there, we found out that there were lots of things we had to do before we could get married. We had to take blood tests and there were lots of papers to fill out for the marriage license.

After we went to the clinic and had our blood drawn and then filled out the papers, Tre said, "Okay, so when are you trying to get married?"

"Well, today is April 8th. So, we're going to do it May 8th."

"What! That's just a month away," he said.

"So what? You said you loved me, right? You said you cared for me, right? So, it shouldn't matter when we get married."

"Well, I thought we were gonna wait til September or something like that."

"Why do we have to wait til September. For what? I'm pregnant with your baby and before this baby is born, we need to be married."

"But...."

"I thought you said you wanted to marry me," I said, challenging him.

"I do! I ain't got an issue with that."

"Okay, then."

"It's just that I was thinking about the money. With it only being a month away I'm only gonna be able to pay a certain amount."

"That's fine. I got money. You got money. Money is not an issue."

For the next month, I planned the wedding of the year. My mom really liked Tre and was happy that we were getting married. She wanted to do everything that she could to help in the planning.

So, the first thing we did was get my dress. We went down to David Bridal's and I found the most fabulous dress. Even though it cost two thousand dollars, I was only going to be married once, so I got what I wanted.

It was when my mother went with me to buy the bridesmaids dresses, that we started talking about who was going to walk me down the aisle.

"I don't know," I said. Even though I saw my father occasionally in Brunswick, he was still using drugs and I knew he wouldn't want to do it.

"Why don't you ask Gerald?" my mother said. "He would love to do it."

I gave my mother a side-eye look. *Gerald?* I still didn't like him, even though I had been trying to be a little better with him. Tre had been talking to me, trying to do what he could to mend that relationship. He kept telling me that Gerald was the man my mom had chosen and that it was really bothering my mom that I didn't have a relationship with her husband.

Tre was right about that. I knew it was hurting my mom that I stayed away—all because of Gerald. She wanted me to be a part of her life and so because of Tre, I tried my best to put on a good face.

But still, I wasn't sure that I wanted Gerald to give me away.

"I don't know about that," I said to my mother.

"But you don't have anyone else, and like I said, he'd love to do it."

I kept thinking that one of my brothers could give me away, but I could hear in my mother's voice how much this would mean to her. She really wanted Gerald to be a part of the wedding and a part of my life.

It was going to take a lot for me to stand next to Gerald in that church, but my mother was right. I didn't have anyone else and I knew this would make her happy.

"Okay," I said.

For the rest of the month, this was the happiest I'd seen my mother and I was glad that I'd agreed to let Gerald do this.

Finally, our wedding day came and Tre and I got married at Hall's Temple and then, we had our reception in Dicksville, a small area that's on the south end of Brunswick. Our reception was at The Port City, a little club, where all seventy-five of us went there and partied! We had such a good time.

The entire wedding cost us thousands and thousands of dollars.

But at the end, I was seventeen, I was married to Tre, and I was really happy about that.

The next morning, when we woke up, I asked Tre, "How much money do you have?"

He shook his head. "I only got two dollars."

I laughed.

"What's so funny?" he asked.

"I only have three dollars. So together, we're starting our married life with five dollars."

Now, we laid up in the bed and laughed together.

"That's okay," Tre said. "We've got five dollars and we have each other."

He was right about that. That's how we started out our married life—broke, happy, and together.

CHAPTER 16

Just a few days after our wedding, I got a telephone call from my mother that was a complete shocker. My grandmother was back!

I had never even met my mother's mother. After my great grandmother took my mother to live with her, my grandmother moved to Chicago. No one had heard from her since, and I'd even heard talk that she might be dead.

I couldn't get over to my Grandmother Lottie's house fast enough. When I got to my great grandmother's house, my grandmother was the first person that I saw. She opened the door with this great big smile on her face.

"You have got to be Shashicka!" she said as if she was as excited to meet me as I was to meet her.

"Yes, ma'am," I said.

"Don't call me ma'am. Call me Susie. I'm your Grandmother Susie."

She hugged me and held me so tightly. Finally, when I stepped back, her eyes looked over me like she was studying everything about me.

I was doing the same thing to her. She was so beautiful to me. Maybe it was because she had this great bubbly personality that I could tell went all the way down to her spirit. She was probably in her early fifties at the time, but she seemed so young.

For the rest of the afternoon, I sat there with my mother, my grandmother, my great grandmother and a whole bunch of other relatives, who came over to see my grandmother. It was like a homecoming, a big ole party. Everyone was just talking and laughing. Everyone seemed okay with my grandmother being there—except for my aunt. My mother's sister was kind of quiet, and sometimes, I would catch her kinda glaring at her mother. I guess she was holding a grudge.

That didn't matter to me because I didn't have anything to do with any problems my aunt, or even my mother had with my grandmother. I was just excited to be able to see *my* grandmother.

I kept quiet most of the time because I just wanted to take in everything I could about my grandmother. It was something to me, I was really a little confused by watching her. All these years, the picture that my mother and everyone else had painted about my grandmother was totally different than what I saw in front of me. She was loving and kind and I couldn't wait to spend even more time with her.

I just had no idea that I would be spending a lot of time with her very soon.

Tre had been making all of his money on the street hustling and now that he stopped, we didn't have that income coming in.

But, I still had my job at the hospital—at least I did for a few weeks after we were married. Then, I was laid off. And without Tre working or dealing and with me not having a job, I didn't know what we were going to do.

Then, about a week after that, more bad news hit us. The light bill came in the mail and when I opened it up, I was shocked—it was over three thousand dollars!

"What is this?" I asked Tre.

He looked at the bill and was just as surprised as I was. "You better call them tomorrow."

That's just what I did. But when I got someone on the phone, the lady told me that my lights were going to be disconnected within the next week if I didn't pay the whole bill.

Since I couldn't get anyone to help me on the phone, I went down to Georgia Power so that I could speak with someone in person. There had to be some mistake. I'd never had a light bill anywhere near one thousand dollars, let alone three.

"This isn't my bill," I tried to explain to the lady who looked at me like she didn't believe me.

"Well, your name is on both accounts."

"Two locations? I only have one apartment." At first I was thinking that she was talking about the apartment I had before. I had paid that bill. "I only have lights at my current apartment."

"What about the lights you have on Johnson Street?"

Now I knew for sure there was a mistake. "I've never lived on Johnson Street so I don't know how I would have a light bill there."

"Well, I don't know what to tell you," the lady said, sounding like she felt a little sorry for me. "But it's in your name, so you're responsible."

I couldn't even imagine who lived on Johnson Street, so I got the exact address and drove right over there. I didn't recognize the house, nothing was familiar.

When I knocked on the door, I couldn't imagine who lived in this place. I figured it was someone that I didn't even know who had used my information.

Then the door opened, and I was shocked. It was Ms. Ethel, the kitchen supervisor at the hospital where I worked.

I didn't even say hello. I just asked, "Who stay here?"

"I stay here!" Ms. Ethel said like she had no idea why I was asking her that question.

"Well, why do you have lights on in my name?" I asked getting straight to the point.

She frowned and then she started shifting her feet. "Well, remember that day when we were in the cafeteria and I was telling you about what was going on in my life?"

I tried to remember what she was talking about. There was one day when she and I were on a break together and she started telling me about her and her husband getting a divorce. But I couldn't figure out what that had to do with her using my name for her lights.

She kept on, "You said that you understood and that if you could do anything to help me, you would."

"I did, but...."

"Well, I thought by you saying that you would help me, you meant it. So, that's when I took it upon myself and I put the lights in your name."

I couldn't believe this! "I didn't tell you that I would help you. I said if I could have done anything to help you, I would. But you never asked me if you could do this."

"Oh, I'm sorry," she said. "I just thought...."

"Well, what are you going to do to resolve this? Because the bill is three thousand dollars and they're getting ready to turn the lights off."

"Well, I'm gonna pay it. I'll just have to make payments."

"I don't think they're gonna give you any time. Georgia Power will be disconnecting the service today 'cause I told them this wasn't me at this address."

"Oh, no," she said. "Well, can you just tell them to let it stay on just a little bit longer?"

"No, I can't. I'm already in trouble with this big bill."

I turned around and went back to my car. By the time I got home, the lights had been disconnected at our apartment. And so I knew Ms. Ethel's lights had been turned off, too.

Tre and I didn't have any choice. We couldn't stay in an apartment without any power and so we had to move. But we didn't have any money, so we ended up moving in, once again, with my great grandmother. Even though the bill wasn't mine, I made payment arrangements to pay off that entire light bill because if I ever wanted to be on my own again, I'd need lights and that account balance had to be zero. Ms. Ethel did make a few payments to help me, though she never did pay her whole part.

Now, we were living with my grandmother and neither one of us had a job. So, Tre went back to hustling. He didn't have any choice. He would stay out all night doing whatever he had to do to make money so that we could get another place.

The only good thing about being with my great grandmother was that my Grandmother Susie was there and being around her always made me smile. Spending that time together allowed us to really get close, though she wasn't there much during the day.

My grandmother worked, and she worked hard. She worked from sun-up to sun-down as a maid. But when she came home, she made that time all about me. My grandmother would have me come into her room and we would just lie on the bed and talk. I could talk to her about any and everything in my life and I had never had anyone that I felt comfortable with like that before. She was truly my best friend and I loved the time that I had there with her.

But, I didn't want to stay with my Grandmother Lottie forever, so while Tre was out hustling, I worked on finding us another apartment. About three weeks after we moved in with my great grandmother, Tre put together a lump sum of money—about three thousand dollars—and I'd found us another apartment, a two-bedroom, one bath, on Reynolds Street.

The apartment was $475 and not only did we have to pay the first month's rent, but we had to give a $475 deposit. The rest of the money, we put on the light bill so that we would have lights at our new place.

Since I had been laid off and was now pregnant, I decided to just stay home and Tre continued to do what he had to do so that we would have money.

But then, about two months before Xavier was born, Tre was arrested for probation violation. He was lucky; he didn't get any jail time, just community service that he had to begin right away.

Tre tried to stay low for the next couple of months, but it seemed to be too hard for him. He just loved being in the streets. And he was in the streets the night that I went into the hospital.

Actually, it had started the day before. I was speaking to my mother on the telephone and telling her just how ready I was to have the baby.

"I'm sick of being pregnant," I said.

"Well, Shicka. Grandma can give you something so that you can hurry up and have the baby."

"What can she give me?"

"She got this tea. Somehow, this tea will dilate your uterus."

"For real?" I couldn't believe that. I'd never heard of anything like that before.

"Yeah. If you want the baby, she can make it happen."

I was only thirty-five weeks, but I was ready. Still, I wasn't sure, so I told my mother that I wanted to think about it, not that I really believed that a tea could really do that.

My mother came over to see me the next day, and we went to my grandmother's house just for our normal visit. When we walked in the door, I yelled out to my grandmother.

"We're here!"

My grandmother came out from her bedroom. "I know you're here. I could hear your mother's old raggedy Mustang the moment you drove up."

I laughed because my grandmother was always teasing my mother about her car.

Then, my grandmother said what she always did, "Darlene, when I'm able, I'm telling you that I'm gonna buy you a brand new car."

"Okay, Mama," my mother said, laughing, too.

When we sat down in the living room, I asked my grandmother about what my mother had told me.

"Grandma, Mama said you could make a tea that can help me have the baby."

My grandmother shook her head. "I ain't giving you no tea. I ain't giving you no tea 'cause you need to wait to have that baby like you're supposed to have that baby."

My mother jumped in. "No, the tea ain't for her. It's for me."

"Oh, okay," my grandmother said. "I'll make it for you."

My mother and I followed my grandmother into the kitchen and we talked about my baby as she made the tea. When she handed the cup to my mother, she said, "Thank you," and pretended like she was going to drink it.

But the minute my grandmother left the room, my mother gave me the cup. "Quick, drink this," she whispered.

I took a sip.

"Hurry up," my mom said, as she looked over her shoulder to make sure that my grandmother wasn't coming back.

The tea was hot, but I drank it as fast as I could.

"Okay," my mom said when I handed her the empty cup. "Now, we've got to walk."

We yelled out to my grandmother, then my mother and I rushed out of the house.

"Why we gotta walk?" I asked.

"Come on, Shicka. This is part of it. You want to have that baby, right?"

I nodded and followed my mother. She made me walk pretty fast. We walked around the block once. Then, a second time.

And my water broke!

"See!" my mother said. "I told you. Let's get to the hospital."

All the way over I couldn't believe it. The tea had worked and now I was going to finally have this baby. But when we got to the hospital and they checked me out, the nurses told us that my water hadn't broken.

"But I felt it," I said.

"No," the nurse told me. "You're not ready yet. We're gonna send you home."

I was so disappointed I could hardly speak.

"I don't know what happened," my mother said. "But don't worry, Shicka. You'll have the baby soon."

When we got to my house, my mother asked, "Where's Tre?"

I shrugged. "I don't know. You know he's out running the streets somewhere."

"Well, I'm going to get going," my mother said. She always liked to get on the road early since she lived an hour away. "You gonna be all right here?"

"Yeah," I said. "I guess I'll just have to wait a couple of more weeks to have this baby."

But just a few hours after my mother left, I felt a contraction. I started to call her, but I waited, thinking about what the nurses had told me earlier. Then a few minutes later, another contraction. And another one. When I checked out my underwear, I was spotting.

Those nurses had been wrong! I was ready to have this baby.

Now what was I gonna do? I had no idea where Tre was and since it was only eight o'clock at night, there was no telling how many more hours would pass before he came home. I wasn't about to sit around and wait for him. And I wasn't gonna call my mom either. She was too far away for me to wait for her. So, I grabbed my purse and car keys and decided that I would just drive myself to the hospital.

About ten minutes later, I was there and this time, the nurses admitted me.

"Yeah, it looks like you're almost ready to have this baby."

After they settled me into the room, I called Tre and was so glad that he answered his phone.

"I'm at the hospital," I told him. "I'm getting ready to have this baby."

"Okay," he said. "I'll be there."

"Are you coming now?"

"Yeah, Shicka. I said I'll be there!"

I hung up feeling satisfied that Tre was on his way. But then an hour passed, and another hour. Just a little more than two hours later, Tre showed up. He busted into the room. Drunk!

"Where's the couch?" he asked me without even saying hello or asking me how I was doing. "I need to lay down."

I just shook my head as he stumbled across the room to the couch. He fell onto the sofa, and then looked at me for the first time.

He said, "You ain't had the baby yet?"

"No!"

Then, he closed his eyes.

He didn't even notice when the nurse would come into the room to check me out. He was just lying there with his eyes closed, his mouth opened, snoring, and making all kinds of noises.

The whole time, my contractions were getting closer and closer and finally about two in the morning, the nurse said, "Okay, I think you're ready. You've dilated ten centimeters."

"Good," I said, "'cause I can't take it anymore. I'm ready to have this baby."

She smiled, then looked over at the couch where Tre had just let out a big snore. She shook her head before she went over and tapped him on his shoulder. "It's time," she told him. "Your baby is about to be born."

Tre's eyes slowly opened up and he groaned. "She wants to have the baby now? She can't hold it until the morning?"

That was it for me! I had been there all night, in pain, ready to have this baby that I didn't want to have, but Tre had talked me into having. And he was gonna say that?

"Tre, if you don't get your...." After that, every curse word that I knew came out of me. "You better help me push this baby out or I know something!"

That seemed to wake my husband right up!

But even though he was up, he wasn't straight. He was still drunk and that was going to end up being a problem for me. Because when they asked Tre to hold my legs up, he pushed my legs so far back, that after I gave birth, I walked with a limp for a couple of weeks. Tre had pulled my legs out of their sockets. Now, I didn't feel it at the time. (Thank God for my epidurall!) But he had me pushed so far back, he hurt me.

The moment I pushed our son out, Tre immediately dropped my legs and went straight to our baby. He was so excited, he seemed to forget all about me.

"Let me see him!" he said to the doctor. "Let me see who he looks like."

Tre and his sister were fussing so much over the baby, I wondered if they remembered me at all.

I didn't have to wonder that for too long, though. Because my husband may have come into the room late and drunk. But once Xavier was born, Tre was there for me the whole time. From the moment we took our son home, Tre stepped up. He was hardly in the streets.

If I didn't see it for myself, I wouldn't have believed it. Our son had changed my husband.

CHAPTER 17

Tre kept the promise that he'd made to me when I agreed to have his child. "When you have my baby, I promise you that I'm gonna be there."

He stayed true to his word.

It was a good thing, too, because after giving birth, that was a hard time for me. I didn't know it at the time, but I think I was going through postpartum depression. I knew I was depressed, and I thought it was mostly because now I had this son, but I didn't have my daughter. It didn't seem fair to LaMiracle. She was my first child, but she couldn't be with me.

But there was also a part of me that didn't want Xavier because since Miracle was with my mom, I was just getting to the point where I was free. And now, I could do a lot of the things that I hadn't had a chance to do since I had LaMiracle so young.

I think Tre kinda figured out what was wrong with me. He could tell that I didn't want to be bothered with our baby. I hated when Xavier cried at night, I wouldn't even get up.

But Tre did. He would get up and feed him and do whatever Xavier needed. If Tre hadn't been there, I don't know what would've happened.

But then, two months after Xavier was born, I got a call one Friday morning and it was Tre. He was calling from jail.

"What happened?"

"I've been arrested."

I couldn't believe this was happening once again, and I had to wait until the next morning to go to the jail to see him during visitation. He told me that he really didn't know why he'd been picked up.

"All they're telling me is that I violated my probation," Tre said.

So two days later, on Monday, I called his probation officer to find out what was going on, and to do my best to get him released.

"Tre was picked up because he hadn't been reporting to me," the probation officer told me. "And not only that, he wasn't doing the community service hours that he'd been given."

"Well, we just had a baby," I told the officer. "Can you get him out and I'll make sure he does what he's supposed to do?"

"No," the parole officer said, shaking his head the whole time. "I'm not going to release him. He's going to have to do the whole ninety days. He'll do his community service while he's in there. He'll be out on work release and he'll have to do the entire five thousand hours."

Well, that meant with Tre being away, even if it was just for ninety days, I was going to have to go back to work. The timing was perfect—the hospital had called and said they had another position for me.

Since I was going to be working and Tre wouldn't be there to help me, my girlfriend, Nicole, moved in with me the day

Tre went to jail. And thank God that she did because she kept Xavier while I worked.

But then, I received some more help from someone that I never expected.

My father.

Over the years, I would see my father around town, but it was always so strange. We would just walk by each other, say hello, and then just keep walking as if we were strangers.

I knew why I treated my dad that way. Even after all of these years, I was still upset and hurt by my father because I always felt like if my father had stayed a part of my life and was still with my mother, then all of the stuff that happened to us would've never happened.

Once I had LaMiracle, though, my dad and I would have short conversations—or rather, he would converse with me. My father would ask me questions and I would answer, but I was always short with him. He'd want to know how was LaMiracle? How was I doing? If things were good with us? I'd just say, "Yes," "No," "We're fine." I just didn't want to be around him, and I didn't want him to be around me.

It wasn't until I got with Tre that I started thinking differently. Tre would always tell me that no matter what, that was my dad.

"You shouldn't treat him that way, Shicka. He's your flesh and blood. He's still your father even if he did get hooked on drugs."

The more Tre talked to me about him, the more I softened. And so, when I ran into my dad a few weeks after Tre was incarcerated, my mindset was different. My heart was ready.

I was coming out of the grocery store and my dad was on his bike. He had to stop or he would've hit me, so we didn't have any choice but to talk.

"Hey," I said.

"Hey, how are you?"

"I'm good," I said.

"And what about Tre and the baby?"

"They're good, too. Tre's away right now, though."

My father seemed really happy that I was there talking to him. So I stayed and told him all that was going on with me—how I was back to work now and still wanted to get custody of LaMiracle. And he told me what was going on with him—how he was staying with some girl, but he wasn't happy so he was looking for a new place to stay.

I hadn't had any kind of relationship with my father for years, but I kept hearing Tre's words in my head. "Well, if you want, you can come and stay with me."

"Really?" He seemed like he was shocked.

I nodded. "While Tre's away, you can help me with the baby."

"I can't believe this," he said with a smile.

"Well, you're my father," I told him. "And, I do love you. You can stay with me."

"So you're not upset anymore?"

I shook my head. "Tre helped me to realize that everything that happened wasn't all your fault." When I gave my father my address, he went right home, got his things and within an hour he was back at my place. I don't know if he got there so fast because he was afraid that I was going to change my mind or if he was just happy to be with me. Whatever it was, that was the beginning of my relationship with my father, and he became a big help and a big part of my life.

So, it was the three of us: me, my father and Nicole there and it didn't take long for me to be really happy that my father was with me. Not only did he help out a lot, but we were able to connect again. Like with my Grandmother Susie, I could talk to my father and it felt like we were making up for all the years we missed out on together. For the first time in my life, I really felt like I had a father.

At first, Nicole was at my place all the time because even though I was getting closer to my father, I didn't always trust him to be alone with Xavier. But as time went on, I didn't see any signs of drugs. Not that I think my father had given drugs up totally, it was just that he never brought that stuff around his grandson. So Nicole was able to go back to her place more, and I relied on my father to help me with Xavier.

He was understanding and caring and he loved us so much. It was a really good time, but the thing was, my father wasn't bringing in any money and now, that was one extra mouth for me to feed. I needed help.

One day I was talking to my cousin, telling her how I'd been struggling and just how hard everything had been. And she told me about the Section 8 program.

"That'll help you a lot with housing, Shicka. You can get a real nice place."

She didn't have to tell me twice—the next day before I went to work, I went downtown and applied for the program. It took about two months, but by the time Tre came home, I had been approved and we moved to Bell Pointe.

My father decided that he didn't want to go with us to Bell Pointe, even though I wanted him, too.

"It's just too far out, baby girl," he told me. "You know where I like to be—in the city."

"I know, but I wish you would come. I like having you with me."

"It's been real good, but just because we won't be living together anymore, doesn't mean we won't be in touch. I'm gonna come out there and see you all the time! Now that I got my baby girl back, I'm gonna spend as much time with you as I can."

I was glad about that. My father living with me during the months that Tre had been away really helped us to reestablish our relationship and I felt as close to him as I did when I was a little girl.

But with Tre home, I didn't have to worry about who would take care of the kids while I worked, so my father not coming with me was okay.

Things got a little bit better for me and Tre. Being on Section 8 helped to relieve some of the financial pressure. And in the meantime, Tre was still hustling and I'd gotten a job at FLETC— Federal Law Enforcement Training Center, which was a much better job than when I'd been working at the hospital. I was earning more, so between my bigger check and Section 8, things were really looking up for us.

The more we earned, the more we got settled. We had caught up on all of our bills and even had a little bit of money saved. One day Tre said, "You know, I think it's time for us to get LaMiracle back. It's been two, going on three years. It's time for you to get your daughter because she needs to be here with us."

I nodded as I listened to Tre. He was so right. I wanted LaMiracle with me so much and I hadn't spent all that much time with her. It was so hard to have her with me then have to give her back to my mother. And it was hard on LaMiracle, too. She would cry every time she had to leave.

So because I hated that and because I felt just a little guilty, I didn't have her around as much as I wanted to. But now, just like Tre had been about Gerald and my father, Tre was right about this, too. I was eighteen now, legally old enough to have my daughter again. And Xavier was a year old; he needed to bond with his sister. They needed that bond with each other.

"Plus," Tre went on, "that will give your mom time to do what she needs to do because raising Miracle is not really her responsibility."

I didn't need any more convincing. My mother had done all that she could, but having LaMiracle with her hadn't been easy. She had to work long hours, twelve-hour shifts, and many times she worked overnight at the hospital. Most of the time she had to leave LaMiracle with Ms. Adeine, a good friend of hers, since I'd made my mother promise that she'd never leave my child alone with Gerald. As much as my mother loved Miracle, it was hard on her when she had to leave Miracle. And, I was sure that it was hard on Ms. Adeine, too. She was an older lady and there was no way she wanted a young child around her all the time.

So after talking to Tre, that night when I got home from work, I called my mom and she told me Miracle was with Ms. Adeine.

"Just tell her you're coming to pick her up," my mother said, sounding happy that I wanted to get Miracle back.

I hung up from my mother and called Ms. Adeine right away. I expected her to be as happy as my mother, but she wasn't.

"Well how long are you taking her for?" she asked. "Is she going to be spending a couple of nights with you or what?"

Her tone was kind of sharp, but I just figured it was because she was surprised to hear from me since I'd never called for LaMiracle before. Whenever I picked up my daughter, I got her from my mother.

"No," I told Ms. Adeine. "I'm coming to take her back."

"Take her back where?"

"Take her back with me. I'm going to raise her now."

"You can't do that because the courts said that she has to stay with your mother."

"No, ma'am, not anymore. I'm eighteen now. I'm grown. I can come get my baby," I said. "I just let my baby stay with my mom until I got old enough and more stable."

"Well, you're not gonna take her."

What was this lady talking about? "What do you mean?" I frowned. Why was this lady giving me a hard time about my child. "That's my baby," I said, "and if you try to keep her from me, I'll call the police if I have to."

That slowed her down just a little bit. "You don't have to do that. I'll call and talk to Darlene. I'll let you take her for a couple of days, but you're gonna have to bring her back."

I decided there was no reason to argue with this lady. She was old, didn't know what she was talking about and nothing she said was going to keep me away. So, I just told her okay and Tre and I went to Jessup to get LaMiracle the next day.

When we picked her up, Ms. Adeine was nicer to me than she'd been on the phone. "Make sure you bring her back now."

I glanced at Tre. "Okay," I told her because like I said, I wasn't going to argue with this lady. This was my daughter.

When I strapped LaMiracle into that car, I felt so good knowing this was the last time that I'd have to pick her up. I'd never have to take her to stay with anyone except for overnight visits. It felt so good to have her with me, so good to know that I was able to take care of her now.

We were young, but being on food stamps and the Section 8 program gave me a lot more stability.

Once she was with us, I went to Social Services so that I could add LaMiracle to my food stamp case so that I could get a little more for her. But the lady told me that wasn't possible.

"Your daughter is already on another case. She can't be on two cases."

That was so weird because my mom hadn't told me that she was getting food stamps for her or LaMiracle. But when I called my mother, she didn't know what I was talking about. She wasn't getting food stamps for anybody.

"Here I go again," I said to myself. Just like with the lights, someone was doing something they weren't supposed to be doing, this time, using Miracle.

So, I went right down to the Department of Family and Children Services to figure out what was going on. I had to show them Miracle's birth certificate and prove that I was her mother. Once they entered all of my information into the computer, they did a search and found out that Ms. Adeine was the one getting the food stamps for LaMiracle. And not only food stamps, she was getting a welfare check for her, too.

But the kicker was, Ms. Adeine was in the process of trying to get full custody of LaMiracle! She had filed papers and everything.

All I kept thinking was that it was a good thing that I'd gone and taken LaMiracle when I did. There's no telling what would've happened if Miracle had stayed with Ms. Adeine even one more day. I would've been in another court fight for sure.

CHAPTER 18

So now, we were all living together and with my job and Tre's hustling, we were getting back on our feet. But while that part of our lives was going well, I didn't feel all that good about my marriage.

I was very suspicious of Tre. Ever since I'd gotten that call from Tasha, I'd been suspicious and I suspected that he was cheating on me. He was hanging out with a bunch of guys who were not married and these guys were all sleeping around with a whole bunch of women. He would come in at all times of the night, sometimes he wouldn't come in until it was almost morning.

We fought about it all the time and the arguments were always the same.

"Why are you coming in at four in the morning?" I'd ask.

"You know why. I'm out hustlin', trying to make money for my family. I've gotta take care of you and the kids."

"Well, what about that girl, Sheila?" Every week, the name changed. There were so many women hanging around Tre and his friends, I couldn't keep track.

"I already told you. Nothing's going on with Sheila or anyone else."

I didn't believe him because if he was out just working, then why didn't he answer my calls whenever I called him at night? I could never reach him after eleven o'clock.

But then, the problem between me and Tre got real.

It was on a Valentine's Day of all days, and when Tre said he wanted to go out to dinner, I was happy because we had been fighting so much, I didn't think he'd want to do anything with me. To me, going out to dinner was a sign that Tre wanted things to be better between us as much as I did.

My brother, Jaime, came over to watch the kids and we went to Outback Steak House and after dinner when Tre gave me a Coach bag and a matching Coach hat for my Valentine's gift, I felt that finally we were on the right track.

On the ride home, Tre said, "I'm going to make a play. You wanna go with me?"

"Sure," I said. I didn't usually go with Tre when he was handling his business in the streets, but this time, I didn't want this night to end. For the first time in a long time, I felt like Tre and I were close again.

When he pulled up in front of our house, he turned off the car. "I've got to run in and get something. I'll be right back." He leaned over and kissed my cheek.

I smiled. This night just kept getting better and better.

The moment Tre went into the house, his cell phone rang. I glanced at the screen and didn't recognize the number. So, I answered it.

"Who's this?" some woman on the other end questioned me.

"I'm Shicka."

"Shicka who?"

"Shicka, Tre's wife."

"His wife? He's with his wife?"

"Yeah, and who are you?"

"I'm Tisha and I've been messing around with Tre for a while."

Inside, I groaned.

She said, "He's supposed to be here with me. It's Valentine's Day."

I couldn't believe I was going through this yet again.

"Where's Tre?" she asked. "Put him on the phone," she demanded like she was the one in charge.

"I'm not gonna do that. Why do you need to talk to him?"

"'Cause when he came over here earlier and gave me my gifts, he told me he would be right back."

I don't know why I asked...I guess I just needed to know. "Gifts? What gifts did he give you?"

"He gave me a Coach bag and a hat! I told you, it's Valentine's Day," she said, as if I didn't know that.

I couldn't believe what Tre had done.

"So, put him on the phone," she demanded again.

"Look, he's my husband and you need to stop calling him." I hung up the phone with an attitude, and then I groaned. Just like I thought, Tre was out there messing around again. And not only had he bought this chick a Valentine's Day gift, but he gave her the same thing that he gave me!

I was in such a daze that I didn't even see Tre come out of the house. It wasn't until he jumped in the car that I realized he was there. "Okay, I'm ready."

Before he could start the car, I said, "So, what's going on with you and Tisha?"

"Who?"

I didn't want to play the game with him where we went back and forth. So, I just got right to it. "She just called you," I said, pointing to his phone.

"You answering my phone?" he asked, like I was the one who had done something wrong.

I ignored him and said, "She told me that she's been seeing you and that you gave her," I stopped and said the rest slowly, "a Coach bag and hat for Valentine's Day."

Tre was quiet and I could tell that he wasn't going to deny it again. "Well, you know, Shicka, I got a lot going on and I'm confused."

"Confused about what?" I asked, suddenly feeling scared. I expected Tre to just deny, deny, deny. And then, when he finally admitted it, I expected him to beg for my forgiveness once again.

But it didn't sound like the conversation was going to go that way.

He said, "Sometimes, I think that we don't need to be together. I got so much that I want to do with my life and you're hindering me from doing what I need to do."

My tears came right away. We'd had a lot of fights over the three years we'd been married about other women, but this was the first time that Tre sounded like he wanted to leave me.

"Why are you saying this?" I cried.

He shrugged. "I don't know, Shicka. It's just not working between us."

"So are you saying that you're going to leave?"

When he didn't answer, I knew that's what he was thinking.

"I don't want you to leave. I really need you here." I felt so weak saying that and crying, but at that moment, that's how I felt. I didn't want my husband to go. I didn't want to give him up to another woman.

"Look," he said as he leaned across and opened the door for me, "I'll talk to you later."

I got out of the car and watched him drive away, leaving me on Valentine's Day. Leaving me there in front of the house.

I knew where he was going. He was going to be with Tisha and as I walked into my house, all I could do was cry. The tears hardly stopped. I was able to hide them from the kids and my brother. But once I was alone in my bedroom, I just let the tears flow. They never stopped. Not even when I got into bed. I couldn't even sleep; I just cried the whole night.

But when seven o'clock came around the next morning, I got up, took my kids to daycare, and went to work like I always did. Even when we were arguing, I never let our arguments nor how Tre acted stop me from doing what I had to do. No matter what, I always went to work. Because I always knew that I had to take care of me. No matter what I felt like, no matter who was doing what, I had to take care of myself and my children.

So, I did what I had to do, but when I came home, Tre was there. He was sitting in the living room, watching television and when I walked in, he said, "Hey," as if nothing had happened the night before.

"Hey," I said. But I didn't say anything else to him. I was really hurt by what he'd done, but like I said before, nothing that Tre was going to do was ever going to stop me from doing what I had to do.

So even though Tre was out in the streets, out in the world, I still got up every day and went to work. He never did leave, even though he didn't change how he was behaving. He was still coming and going whenever he wanted to, staying out to all hours of the night.

We didn't argue as much about it anymore. I guess I just gave up. There was nothing I could do or say to change what he was going to do anyway.

But about three months after that Valentine's Day, I got another call.

"This is Tisha," she said when I picked up the phone. "I'm just calling to let you know that I'm pregnant." Then, she hung up.

I wasn't sure how she got my number. Probably looking through Tre's phone. But whatever, she had my number, she called me, and I knew she had called me because she was hoping that I would put Tre out. And, I did. When I got home, I told Tre that he had to leave.

"She's pregnant," I screamed at him. "I can't believe it, but Tisha is pregnant!"

"Nah, nah, I don't know why she's saying that," he said.

"Well, I believe her. She wouldn't say that she was pregnant if she wasn't."

"If she's pregnant, then the baby's not mine."

"You still got to get out of here."

"You want me to leave?" he asked. "You're gonna believe her over me?"

I couldn't believe he was really asking me that. He hadn't given me a reason to believe him about anything. "Look, if she's pregnant with your baby, then I don't want you here."

He stomped out of the house like he was mad at me, but while he was gone, I packed up all of his clothes. He was shocked when he came home and saw the bag.

"I can't do this anymore," I told him. "You got to go."

"That girl's baby is not mine. I told you."

I just shook my head. "I can't, Tre. I can't."

When he saw that I was serious, he finally took his bag. But before he walked out the door, he tried to convince me one more time.

"I don't care," I said. "You have to go."

And he finally left.

Even though I was the one who had asked him to leave this time, I was so hurt. I was so hurt that he was gone and I was so hurt by what he'd done. My husband was having a baby by somebody else. I never thought this would happen to me.

But even though my heart was hurt, I did what I always did. I kept going. I wasn't ever going to let hurt stop me from what I had to do.

Even though Tre left that day, he kept coming back. Over the next few weeks and months, Tre called all the time, or he would stop by just so that we could talk.

Tre would always say the same things. "That baby's not mine, Shicka. I love you, I don't love that girl."

Every time, I fell for it. Tre would come home and we would be fine. But then after a few days, it would start up all over again. Tre would be back in the streets and I knew he was with Tisha. I would get fed up and put him out again. But the cycle would start all over again. He would call, we would talk, he would come back.

After a few months, though, everything changed. Tisha called me asking for Tre and she told me, "I know he's telling you that this isn't his baby. But that's not what he's saying to me."

When Tre came home, I asked him about it. "You keep saying the baby isn't yours," I said. "Are you sure?"

For the first time, Tre shook his head. "I'm not sure, Shicka. I think the baby is mine."

I didn't think it was possible, but that admission broke my heart even more. Not only because he finally admitted it, but I was hurt because of why he was saying that. All of this time, he'd been denying it, but I felt that now, he was admitting it because he really wanted to be with Tisha.

Up to this point, I guess I was able to take it because I kept telling myself that there was a good chance that the baby wasn't Tre's. But now that he was admitting it, I really couldn't take it.

"You need to leave," I said.

Those were the same words that I always said, but Tre knew that this time I meant it. And I guess he meant it too, because this time when he walked out that door, he didn't come back. He stayed away. He didn't come back home.

I missed Tre, I really did, but I did everything I could to stay away from him. I didn't even allow him to see the kids because I was so hurt. I had a feeling that he did see LaMiracle and Xavier whenever they were with my mom. She would never keep him away from them. But he never saw the kids when they were with me.

The hurt I was feeling made me even more motivated to do something bigger and better with my life. I didn't know what I was going to do, but I knew that something was out there for me. It didn't matter that Tre wasn't going to be a part of my life anymore.

One of the first things I wanted to do was buy the house that I was living in. I had saved quite a bit of money and when I spoke to the landlord, she told me that she would sell me the house.

"But you might want to go take some classes first," she said. "They have these classes downtown that will help you with your credit. After you do that, I'll help you get this house."

It was only a two-week class, but as soon as I finished, I called my landlord and like she promised, she helped me. She referred me to the mortgage broker and after what felt like a long, two-month process, I was able to qualify for the house. I bought my first piece of property. I was only twenty years old.

So, that became my life. Just working and taking care of my kids. I did spend a lot of time with my Grandmother Susie whenever I could and her talks really helped me to get through the hard times.

"I really hope you and Tre can find a way to work it out," my grandmother said.

But I didn't think that was going to be possible. I didn't even know where Tre was staying, and I didn't care. I suspected that he was with Tisha, but there was nothing I could do about that. My thing was, I was never going to be with a man who had a baby on me.

Then, tragedy came into my family. Something that would change my life, something that was so horrible.

But then, just like God always does, he took something bad and turned it into good. And because of what was about to happen, my life would be forever changed.

CHAPTER 19

It had been a long journey for my Grandmother Susie. She'd had cancer for several years, but when she was told that she had to go to a hospice because she only had about six months to live, my mother decided that it was time for my grandmother to come live with her.

"Is she going to be all right?" I asked my mother when she told me that she was moving my grandmother in with her.

"She has cancer, Shicka. It's eaten up her uterus, her kidneys, most of her organs. She can't take care of herself anymore."

My mother hadn't answered my question and that's when I knew it had to be real bad. I was shocked. Like I said, we'd known my grandmother had had cancer for a couple of years, but I didn't realize that it had affected so much of her. Really, I had tried not to think about it because it felt like I'd just met my Grandmother Susie and I wasn't trying to think about losing her so soon.

"Okay," I told my mother, "I'm going to help you take care of her. You won't have to do that all by yourself."

When I got off the phone, I was so upset. My Grandmother Susie meant everything to me and I just couldn't imagine what I would do if anything happened to her. I was determined to do anything I could to help my mother. I was determined to help my grandmother be as happy and as comfortable as she could be as she went through this.

Every one of my off days and every time I could find the time, I went out to Odum to help my mother and be with me grandmother. Sometimes, I would take the kids with me, and sometimes, Tre would watch them for me.

Tre and I weren't back together, but when he found out about my grandmother, he started coming back around and being there for me. I never asked him who told him about my grandmother, I just figured it was my mother. But I never asked him because it really didn't matter. I still wasn't thinking about Tre.

About a month after my mother moved my grandmother in with her, Tre came home for good. He just moved back in. He didn't ask and I didn't ask what he was doing there. We never talked about it, he just came home one day, stayed, and never left.

When I told my mother that Tre was back, she said that was good.

"I told him that he needed to go home," she said. "I told him that you were his wife and that the house belonged to the both of you, so you couldn't just put him out."

I wasn't mad at my mother for talking to Tre, but as far as he was concerned, I just didn't care. Whenever it came to anything that had to do with Tre, I pushed those thoughts out of my mind and just focused on my life. I wasn't going to let him and all of that nonsense bring me down. But even though Tre had taken me through a lot, I have to admit, he was right

there by my side with my grandmother. That was more way more than I could say about Gerald.

From the moment my mother took her mother in, Gerald was never there. He had started messing around with some woman in Waycross and never came home. So, my mom was by herself, through all of those bad times. Grandmother Susie was getting sicker by the day and not even her mother, Grandmother Lottie was there. I didn't understand Gerald, but I could understand Grandmother Lottie not being there. Grandmother Lottie was old and it had to be hard to watch your child deteriorate the way Grandmother Susie was deteriorating.

So my mother was all alone except for the times when I could get out there to help. My grandmother did have a little bit of insurance that allowed a nurse to be there some days, but for the most part, my mother took care of her mother by herself. I already didn't like Gerald and I never forgave him for that.

A few months after my grandmother was with my mother, my mother called and told me that my grandmother wanted to see me.

"She wants to get all the kids together for her birthday. She wants to see everyone one last time."

Those words—one last time—really upset me. But when I told Tre, he helped me keep it together.

"Let's get out there for her, Shicka."

So, the next morning, we packed up the kids and drove out to Odum. We were able to stay for two days, since it was the weekend and I was off.

But this time while I was out there, I came to the realization that my grandmother really didn't have much time left. For one thing, I saw how the cancer had started to eat away at her skin. When I went to change her, my grandmother didn't have any bottom at all.

There was just a big hole where I could actually just look up into my grandmother's body.

That made me so sick. Not because of what it looked like but because I knew the pain that my grandmother was in. Whenever she urinated or had a bowel movement, she would scream in excruciating pain. She was really suffering.

For those two days, I did everything in my power to make my grandmother comfortable. I took over as much as I could from my mother. Tre helped, too, and that really helped to give my mother a little bit of a break. But the best thing was that it gave me a lot of time with my grandmother.

I hardly left her room; Tre and I even slept in her room. We were in her bed while she slept in her hospital bed. I hardly wanted to leave, not even to go to the bathroom. I wasn't going to say it out loud, but my heart knew that she didn't have very much money left.

All I did was love on my grandmother. I sat with her and I talked to her. She had stopped responding, but I knew in my heart that she heard every word that I said and she understood me. We had been so close that we didn't need words. Grandmother Susie had always said that I was like a daughter to her. And I know I was...I was the daughter that she never raised.

When Sunday night finally came and it was time for me to leave, I didn't want to go. I was so scared. Suppose this was the last time that I would see her?

But Tre kept encouraging me. "We'll be back, Shicka," he kept saying. "We'll be back in a couple of days."

I helped Tre pack up and put our bags in the car and then, I went back in the house. When I went into her bedroom, I was glad that Tre already had the kids in the car. I just wanted it to be me and her.

I stood in the doorway for a moment, just watching my grandmother sleep. For some reason, I just knew that this could be the last time. So, I wanted to study her and take in every part of her so that I would always remember.

Then, I walked slowly to her bed. I stood over her for a moment before I leaned over. "Grandma, I love you so much," I whispered to her. "I know how sick you are, and I know that you're going to have to leave me. But, I want you to know that no matter what, you're always going to be a part of my life. I promise you."

I had to stop for a moment because I was so full of emotions. And when I stopped, a single tear pressed out of my grandmother's eye and rolled down her cheek.

With my thumb, I gently wiped the tear away. "It's okay, Grandma," I said. "I know you're hurting," I said, thinking about how the cancer had literally eaten away at her. "And I don't want you to hurt no more. So it's okay to go. I get it. I'll miss you, but I get it and I will always love you."

The more I talked to my grandmother, the louder her breathing became. Actually,it sounded more like wheezing. As she breathed, I heard a rattling sound coming from her chest. I stayed with her for a few more moments, but then Tre came to the door.

"Shicka," he said softly. "We have to go. It's really raining hard and it's gonna take longer to get home."

I had tears in my eyes when I kissed my grandmother's forehead. Finally, "Okay, Grandma. I'm fixn' to go home, but I'll be back tomorrow. As soon as I get off from work, I'll be back here to see you."

It still took me a little bit of time to walk out of that room, but I finally did. I hugged my mother, then Tre got the kids inside the car. It was a quiet ride. Because of the rain, it took us double the amount of time to get home. And on the whole drive back, all I could do was think about my grandmother.

The moment we walked into the house, my cell phone rang and before I even answered it, I knew.

"Shicka," my auntie said. "She's gone."

Even though I had already known in my heart that tonight was the last time I'd see her, that didn't stop my heart from breaking. That didn't stop me from screaming when my aunt said those terrible words—she's gone.

"Why God? Why?" I kept saying over and over. "Why did you take her?"

I had told my grandmother that it was okay for her to go, but I was just saying that for her. I didn't want her to leave. What was my life going to be like without her?

The first time I screamed, Tre came running into the room. "Oh, my God," he said, already knowing what happened without me even telling him. He did his best to comfort me. "Calm down, Shicka. Your grandmother is at peace now."

"I know," I said, "but I have to go see her."

Tre nodded. "We'll go in the morning."

"No! I want to go out there tonight."

"No," he said strongly as if he was putting his foot down. "It's raining and I know you wouldn't want anything to happen to the kids. We'll go in the morning. I promise I'll take you in the morning."

Tre got the kids in bed because I couldn't do it. All I could do was do was stay in my bedroom and cry. I didn't even sleep that night, I was too sick with grief. I hurt from a pain that I'd never felt before. I hurt from a pain that I'd never thought would go away. My grandmother had been gone for just an hour and already I missed her so much.

The next morning, I called into FLETC and told my boss what happened. Then, Tre got the kids ready and just like he promised, he drove me back out to Odum. When we got there, my mother was so shaken up, I was scared for her. I asked my aunt if anyone had called Gerald.

"I did," she said. "But I couldn't reach him. I guess he's still with that woman."

I couldn't believe that Gerald hadn't even come back for this. His wife had just

lost her mother and he was still out there messing around. My prayer was that one day he would pay for the way he'd treated my mother all of these years. I hoped that one day he would pay for not being the husband that he should've been—especially at a time like this.

My mother had gone into her bedroom and I followed her in there. When she saw me, she held her arms out and I fell into her embrace. We just held each other and cried together.

I could feel my mother's exhaustion. All this time, she'd given up everything that she wanted to have or wanted to do to take care of my grandmother. She'd given so much and she was tired.

When I finally pulled back from her, I said, "Mama, I promise you, you ain't gonna want for nothin' no more. I'm gonna take care of you from now on."

I meant every word I said. My mother had touched my heart with the way she'd taken care of her mom, and now, I made a promise that I was going to do the same for her.

It took a few years, but I was finally able to do something for my mother that my grandmother had always promised her. I was able to get my mother a new car.

When I gave her the keys to her new Dodge Neon, my mom thanked me. But I told her that this gift didn't come from me.

"It wasn't me, it was your mom."

My mother frowned.

"You don't remember grandmother telling you that she was going to do this? She was able to get that done through me."

My mother hugged me and every few years after that, I bought my mother a new car.

All because of my grandmother.

CHAPTER 20

Tre stood by me the whole time my grandmother was sick and when she passed away, he was still there. The way he treated me and cared for me, made me rethink all of the thoughts that had been going through my mind about him all of these past months. It was very clear to me that whatever problems we had, Tre really loved me.

But Tre coming home didn't solve the problem I had with him and other woman. There was of course, Tisha. For the first few years after Tre came back, Tisha would call all the time, doing everything she could to get Tre to come back to her. She would call when the baby needed diapers, she would call when something went wrong in her house, she would call to tell me that she and Tre were still messing around.

But the big blow came when Tisha moved to Augusta. I was thinking that things would finally settle down with her, that she would finally leave us alone. But I was wrong because a few days after she moved, Tre got a letter in the mail: a demand to pay child support.

"I can't believe she did this," he said.

"Well, she did. And she's not going to stop. She's going to keep it up, and I don't want her affecting our life, our marriage, and what we're trying to build. But before you give her anything, you need to go get a blood test ."

"You got that right," he said.

The next day, he went down to the Social Services department and spoke to the case manager that had been assigned to Tisha's claim. Tre told her that he wanted a blood test before he paid anything, and the case manager agreed. A blood test was set up; Tisha even had to come back from Augusta and everyone took the test. Three weeks later, the results were in—the child was not Tre's!

For three years, Tisha had passed that baby off as my husband's thinking that he would stay with her because of that. I was amazed that she really thought that would work. But once we found out, that Tre wasn't the father, Tisha was out of our lives for good. It felt great to finally be able to move on.

The only problem...it was difficult to move on because Tisha might have been the first woman to claim that Tre was the father of her child, but unfortunately for me, Tisha wouldn't be the last.

CHAPTER 21

L osing my grandmother had left a void in my life, but it really helped that Tre was back home. He was so supportive, so caring when I needed that the most and for a while, my life was very good, even though I truly missed my Grandmother Susie.

I was still working at Federal Law Enforcement Training Center in registration, processing the students who came into the center, getting all of their information: their address, social security numbers, everything that was needed to enroll them into the school. After that, I'd give them their ID badge, and give them all the information they needed for their classes.

Every FLETC office had to have an officer who patrolled the center to make sure that nothing was going on. On the weekends, Rhonda Coleman was the officer assigned to be with me.

We became kinda friends, at least at work. We would talk about what was going on in our lives. I would talk about my husband and our kids, and Rhonda would talk about her boyfriend. I was surprised when she told me that she had a boyfriend because I had always suspected that she messed around with her boss, who was a sergeant. I didn't know that for sure, though. And since Rhonda never mentioned it, I didn't either.

Rhonda also told me how well she was doing financially. She was making about $15 an hour, which was great back in 2000 and on top of that, she was getting a social security check from her grandmother, so she was well off for someone her age.

Since it was just the two of us (and her boss) together on the weekends, I would make the lunch runs because officers couldn't leave the premises. While I was out, if any students came into the building, the sergeant told Rhonda that she could go into the computer and get all the information so that the students wouldn't have to wait for me.

Rhonda and I worked together for about eight months before we kind of had a falling out. We didn't get into any kind of argument or anything. It was just that I found out that Rhonda was pregnant and she had told everyone who worked in our building not to tell me. Rhonda was telling everyone that she was pregnant by her boyfriend, but when I heard the news, I really suspected that the sergeant was her baby's father. Maybe that was why Rhonda didn't want me to know. Maybe she knew that I would be suspicious of who was the real father. But either way, I felt that she should have told me instead of talking about me behind my back and from that point, I stopped dealing with her.

A few months after that, though, things really heated up. I'd been home from work for just about an hour when I heard a knock on the door. When I opened it, a man and a woman was standing there. Even though they didn't have on uniforms, I knew that they were some kind of police.

"May I help you?" I asked them.

"Are you Shashicka Hill?"

"Yes, how can I help you?" I repeated.

"We're Federal Agents," the man said as they stepped inside. "We're doing an investigation." He handed me some papers. "We have a search warrant and we need to look around your home."

"For what?" I asked as I quickly tried to check out the papers he gave me.

"We're looking for something," the female agent said.

The first thing that came to my mind was what in the world had Tre done? He was still in the streets, doing things that he shouldn't be doing. But I could not imagine what he had done that would have Federal Agents coming to our house.

There was nothing I could do. I had to let them in and let them look around because they had the papers. But the whole time, I watched them and wondered what was going on. The search wasn't long—just five or ten minutes.

The female agent said, "We don't see anything here."

"Well, can you tell me what's going on? What are you looking for?"

The agents looked at each other and then the woman explained. "You work with Rhonda Coleman, correct?"

"Yes," I said as I frowned. Rhonda's name was the last name I expected the agents to say.

Now, I had no idea at all what this was about. Why were they in my home if this had something to do with Rhonda? And what could she have done that involved Federal Agents?

"Well, she's been involved with credit card theft and fraud," the female agent explained to me.

"What?" I said, shocked. That didn't even sound right. Why would Rhonda get involved in something like that with all the money she made?

Then, the agent really shocked me when she said, "And Rhonda told us that you were involved with this, too."

"What? I'm not involved with anything like that and I don't believe Rhonda is either."

Then, the agents broke it down to me. It seemed that Rhonda was taking the social security numbers and other information of the students from my computer. Then, she used that information to apply for credit cards, and then use the credit cards to buy things like computers, televisions and other electronics.

"Are you serious?" I asked the agents. It all just seemed so crazy to me; I just couldn't believe it.

"Yes. So far, she's ordered over forty thousand dollars worth of equipment."

"My God!" All I could do was shake my head because none of this made sense.

"And she said you're involved in this, too," the female agent repeated. But then, she looked around. "One thing, though. Where's your computer? We saw the old one in your bedroom but we don't see another one."

"That's the only computer I have. All I can say is that I don't know anything about what's going on."

The agents looked at each other, then nodded. "Okay. Well, we have to complete our investigation, but we'll get back to you."

The female agent handed me her card and I looked at it. She said, "Call me if you have any questions or if there is anything that you can add to help us."

"Okay," I said, even though I knew I wouldn't be calling her. I couldn't help her if I didn't even know what she was talking about.

For the rest of the night, I couldn't stop thinking about what those agents had said. At first, I was going to call Rhonda, but I decided not to. We hadn't really spoken to each other in a while, and I knew this was nothing but a mistake anyway.

But then the craziness got even worse when I went into work the next morning. As soon as I got there, my supervisor called me into her office.

"I know you've heard about the investigation," she said. "About what's going on with Rhonda."

"Yeah," I said, sitting down in front of her desk. "I couldn't believe it. I can't believe she's involved in that stuff."

I thought my supervisor was going to tell me that she couldn't believe it either. But when she said, "Well, they say that you were involved in this also," I knew this conversation wasn't going to go the way I wanted.

"I'm not!" I told her. "I'm not involved in nothing like this."

She shook her head. "Rhonda says that you are and we can't have you working here if you're involved in theft."

"But, I'm not," I repeated again, wanting to make sure that she heard me.

She shook her head. "I'm sorry, but we're going to have to put you on suspension until further notice."

"So you're telling me that I'm not going to be paid? For how long?"

"I don't know. We won't be able to bring you back here until the investigation is over."

"I can't believe you're doing this," I said, trying hard not to cry. "I keep telling you that I didn't do anything!"

"I'm sorry," was all she said before she told me that I had to leave the building.

I went home kind of in a daze. How could this be happening? What was going on? I didn't know a thing and I was pretty sure that Rhonda didn't know either.

And even if Rhonda was involved, why would she even put me in the middle of something that I didn't have any idea about? None of this made any sense. I just didn't believe the Federal Agents, and I didn't believe my supervisor. All of them had the wrong girl.

When I got home, I told Tre what was going on. I hadn't said anything the day before because I was kinda sure that by today, it would all be cleared up. But now that I was suspended from my job, I had to tell him.

"Can you believe they think I'm involved?" I asked Tre when I finished telling him the whole story.

He was quiet for a couple of seconds. "Well, are you sure you didn't do anything?"

"No! I didn't," I said with an attitude. "How could you even ask me that?"

He held up his hands as if he wanted me to calm down. "I'm just saying, there has to be a reason why they would think you had something to do with it. And you do hang out with Rhonda a lot."

I couldn't believe Tre thought that. That was the kind of thing he would be involved in—not me. At least when I told my mother, she believed me.

"Oh, my God," she said after I told her the story. "But don't worry, Shicka. You didn't have anything to do with that and because of that, God will work it all out. He always does and then they'll find out that you're innocent."

My mother did make me feel a little better, but when I woke up the next morning and realized that I wasn't going to work, I felt even worse. As I sat around the house, I got more depressed and knew that I had to do something. I decided it was time for me to speak to Rhonda myself.

When I called and she answered, I got straight to the point without even saying hello. "Rhonda, what is going on?"

"What are you talking about?" she answered innocently as if she didn't know what I was talking about.

So, I broke it down for her. "Look, these people came to my house, they said you did this credit card fraud thing and that you put me in it."

"No, that's not true! I don't know what's going on." She sounded like she was shocked. "They were talking to me, too, but I have no idea what they're talking about 'cause there's nothing going on."

"They just suspended me because of this investigation and I don't think they would be doing all of this if something wasn't going on."

"Yeah, they did the same thing to me, too, but I never said that you had anything to do with it."

"Well, okay, then," I said. If she was involved, she wasn't going to admit anything and I wasn't going to get anywhere staying on the phone. Plus, she did sound sincere to me. It did sound like Rhonda had no clue what was going on. "I'll talk to you later."

As soon as I hung up, I found the female agent's card so that I could talk to her and tell her what I found out from Rhonda.

But before I could tell the agent everything that Rhonda said, she stopped me.

"Listen, this situation is real no matter what she says. We're not lying. Rhonda is involved in credit card fraud and she did put you in this. You need to understand that we are not investigating you for nothing. We're going through the phone records, we're going through everything to find out the truth. We're gonna find out if you're involved. And if you are, you're going to prison. Because this is serious, this is a federal offense."

The entire time she was talking, my heart was beating so fast. Prison? A federal offense? What was I going to do? What would happen to my children?

I hung up the phone not sure of what to do next. I was so scared. I knew I hadn't done anything wrong, but supposed something went wrong? I just had to believe that I was innocent and they would figure that out.

In the meantime, though, I had immediate problems—like how was I going to pay my bills until all of this got cleared up.

Tre had a plan. "Just give me your check," he told me.

It was my last check and I wasn't sure that I wanted to give it to him. "What are you gonna do?"

"I'm gonna flip it."

I didn't know exactly what that meant, but I knew it had something to do with Tre hustling. So, I gave it to him. And he flipped it. And we had money for the next couple of weeks.

I couldn't believe how the days turned into weeks and then it was a month. Just when I was beginning to wonder how much longer this was going to take, I got a call. When the female agent said, "Hello," I recognized her voice right away. My hand started trembling so much, I could hardly hold the telephone.

"Shashicka, we wanted to get back to you. We completed our investigation."

"Okay," I said. I knew I hadn't done anything wrong, but her voice didn't sound happy.

She said, "We came to the conclusion that you had no contact with Rhonda. I don't understand why she put your name in it. But we're releasing you from the investigation."

I felt like I was breathing for the first time in a month. "Thank God!" I said, truly relieved.

"I'm sorry you had to go through all of this," the agent said, "but during the investigation, Rhonda finally explained it all to us. You didn't know this, but she would go into your computer whenever you stepped away from your desk and she would get all of the students' information.

All I could think about was all of those times when Rhonda would send me out to get lunch for everyone. Now, I knew why. I just couldn't believe it, but I thanked the agent and sat down in the living room, just thinking about what had happened. Thank God Rhonda finally told the truth.

About five minutes later, the phone rang again.

"Shashicka!" It was my boss. "We just heard that you're being released from the investigation," she said sounding happy, too. "So you can come back to work."

For thirty days, I had waited for this phone call, but when she said that, I just sat there. For the first time, I wasn't afraid, now I was just hurt. I had been working at that job for two years and in all that time, I had worked hard. I had never done anything wrong, hardly made any mistakes and had been to work every day. My boss knew that and she knew me. She knew how I worked, she knew I wouldn't have been involved in anything like that. So, she should've believed me.

But she didn't. She put me on a suspension without ever really listening to my side of the story.

So, I said the first thing that came to my mind. "I'm not coming back."

My supervisor paused for a moment. "Really? Why not?"

I didn't feel like explaining it to her, so all I said was, "You just need to get someone else."

When I hung up, I felt good about my decision. Even though I didn't know what I was going to do, I wasn't going to go back to a job where my boss wouldn't give me the benefit of the doubt. I wasn't going to work with anyone who didn't trust my word.

Rhonda ended up doing two years behind this and the whole time, all I could do was thank God. Because I could have easily gotten involved with Rhonda. Not that I would've done anything illegal, but she was buying electronics and reselling them. And, at that time, I'd wanted a computer so bad that if she had asked me, I probably would've bought one from her. Then, I would have been caught up in all of that. I might not have been able to clear my name.

It was a nightmare for Rhonda, and it could have been a nightmare for me. Except God helped me to turn what could have been a nightmare into a dream. Because of being suspended from my job, I was on my way to becoming a millionaire.

CHAPTER 22

Now that I had decided that I wasn't going to go back to the Federal Law Enforcement Training Center, I had to find a new job. I didn't know what I was going to do, so I did what I always did when I had a problem—I talked to my mom.

"Well, I think you should think about doing what I'm doing," my mother told me. "It's really easy."

I kinda rolled my eyes a little. My mother had been working with the nurse who'd helped us take care of my grandmother. She had other cases and she had hired my mom to help her out with other people who needed home health care.

My mother said, "Shicka, it's really good, it's really easy. All I do is sit with these people. That's it. You already said that you liked doing it with Grandma."

Yeah, I did like taking care of my grandmother, but she was my grandmother. I really enjoyed those times with her, but I wasn't so sure that I would feel the same way about a stranger. "I don't know if I want to do that, Mama."

After I had that talk with my mom, though, I couldn't stop thinking about it. I really did love taking care of my grandmother and I was thinking that I could help other elderly people the way I'd helped her.

But the more I thought about it, the more I began to think that wasn't for me. I was used to working in an office. I had worked in a hospital before, but it was in the cafeteria, not with the patients. I wasn't used to going into someone's home. And even if I did work with the nurse that my mother was working with, how was I ever going to turn that into a full-time job?

A few days later, my mother talked to me about it again. "I really think you should do it, Shicka. Just put an ad in the paper and see what happens."

I couldn't figure out what else I was going to do, so I decided to try it. I placed an ad in the newspaper and got a call the next day.

The call came from a woman named Emily who lived on Sea Island. "I was really glad to see your ad," she said. "I have a very good friend who needs twenty-four hour care and I'm not able to be there for her the way she needs me to because I have to work."

"Okay," I said. "What does she need?"

"Well, she's in the hospital right now and I'd like someone to be there with her. But in a couple of weeks, she'll be going home and we'll really need someone with her then."

"Does she have any family?" I asked.

"No, she's a widow. I have her power of attorney and I would be the one paying for her care."

"Okay," I said again. "I can do it, but I can't do it for twenty-four hours. You'll have to find someone else."

"Well, I don't know anybody, so I tell you what. Why don't you just find the people to work for the twenty-four hours and I'll pay you and you can pay them."

I thought about that for a moment and it sounded good to me, so I told Emily that I would take the job.

Like she told me, her friend, Ms. Neil was in the hospital, and Emily wanted someone to sit with her all day and all night.

That seemed easy enough to me. I did the seven to three shift, my mom did three to eleven and another lady that I'd hired did the night shift. We did that for about two weeks and then, Ms. Neil was released from the hospital.

"I can't be there to take her home, so can you do it?" Emily asked me the day before Ms. Neil was released.

"Sure." I was getting paid for it so I didn't mind.

I got my mom to go with me and with the help of the nurses, we got Ms. Neil into the car. Ms. Neil was about seventy years old and the cancer she had made her very weak. There wasn't much that she could do to help herself, so I knew that once we got her home, the real work would begin.

When we were all in the car, I called Emily to find out exactly where Ms. Neil lived. "We need directions so we can take Ms. Neil home."

"She knows where she lives," Emily said. "She can tell you where she lives, and like I told you last night, the key is under the mat."

"Okay."

I knew how to get to Sea Island and once there, I asked Ms. Neil which way to go.

She started giving me directions. "Make a left," she said. Then, at the next block, she said, "Make a right. Now, go straight." I drove for a little while, making all kinds of turns. "At the stop sign, make another left."

Finally, after a few minutes, we were right on the edge of the ocean.

There were houses on the left and on the right. "So, where do you live?" I asked, expecting her to tell me to turn left or right.

But Ms. Neil pointed straight ahead. She pointed to the water. "That's where I live."

I looked over at my mom. What was this lady talking about? She lived on the ocean?

"Do you live in any of these houses?" I asked, pointing.

She shook her head. "No. I stay out there," she said, like she was sure she lived on the water.

Okay, this was not going to work. Emily needed to give me directions. I got her on the phone and told her what Ms. Neil was saying.

"She keeps telling us that she lives on the ocean."

Emily busted out laughing. "Let me speak to her."

I handed Ms. Neil the phone and even though she had the phone pressed to her ear, I could hear Emily's voice.

"Why aren't you telling the ladies where you live?" Emily asked.

"That's where I live!" Ms. Neil insisted.

"Lucy, stop it. They're trying to take you home."

"That's where I live," she kept saying.

Finally, I took the phone away from her and asked Emily what she wanted me to do. "'Cause right now, we're sitting out here in the car in front of the ocean and we don't know where to go."

"I don't know why she's kidding with you guys. Okay, let me tell you."

I wondered why she hadn't just given us the directions from the beginning, but I just did what she told me to do and within five minutes, we were there. It took some time for my mom and I to lift Ms. Neil out of the car. And just like Emily said, the key was under the mat.

I opened the door, stepped inside, and froze. I felt like I was in the middle of an old black and white movie back in the 1800's. Every piece of furniture, every picture, everything in the place was black or white, and oversized and old! I didn't think they made chairs and tables like this anymore.

I had never been in a house like this before. Everything was ancient-looking. looking like it was at least two-hundred years old. And it felt like there were spirits in the house. It felt as if the people who used to sit in those chairs and sit at those tables were right there. It was just really spooky.

The house was so cold that I was shivering. And even though it was daylight outside, it was as if the sunshine didn't want to come through and shine on all of that old stuff.

I turned on a couple of lamps, but even with the inside light, it was still really dim. "I don't like lights," Ms. Neil told me.

While my mother took Ms. Neil into her bedroom, I called Emily to tell her that we'd finally gotten Ms. Neil settled. But, when I spoke to her, I just had to tell her that the house seemed so strange to me.

"Everything is so old," I said.

"Yeah, that furniture had been handed down to Ms. Neil from her grandparents. Just get her into bed and she'll probably sleep for the rest of the day."

"Okay," I said.

I checked on my mother and she already had Ms. Neil in the hospital bed that had been set up in her bedroom.

"I'm gonna go," my mother said. "I'll be back to relieve you at three."

As I walked my mother to the door, I wanted to tell her not to leave me. Right before she stepped outside, she whispered, "It's so spooky in here."

"I know," I said, wishing that my mom would stay.

But she walked right out the door, leaving me alone. At least she would be back in a few hours and I'd be able to get out of there.

I went back toward Ms. Neil's bedroom and as I walked down the hallway, I could feel the eyes of the people in all those old pictures on the wall looking at me. I was so glad to get to her bedroom.

"Ms. Neil, are you hungry?" I asked her.

She nodded her head just a little.

"Okay, I'm going to make you lunch and I'll be right back."

She nodded again, and I walked out of her bedroom. I had to pass all those pictures again, with the eyes following me. In my head, I knew that every person in those old pictures was dead, but I could swear that they were all watching me from wherever they were now.

Even though it was scary, I still had a job to do.

At least Emily had stocked the kitchen with food, so that was good. I made lunch, took it to Ms. Neil, then sat in the bedroom with her. But, I couldn't wait for my mother to come back and when I heard that doorbell ring, I jumped up, ran to the door, hugged my mother and then, I got out of there real quick.

Of course, I was back there the next morning, relieving the friend of my mother's that I had hired to do the overnight shift with Ms. Neil. When I got there, I made Ms. Neil a cup a coffee and gave her the medication. She seemed even weaker that morning; she could hardly lift her head to drink. So, I just let her lay in the bed.

After a few minutes, Ms. Neil closed her eyes and fell asleep. I just stayed in the room, flipping through magazines. The house was so quiet, but I tried not to think about that. Then, after a few minutes, I heard that sound. That same rattling sound coming from her chest as she breathed. It was the same sound that I'd heard with my grandmother.

I stood up and slowly walked to the bed so that I could see if Ms. Neil was all right. Her eyes were closed, but that rattling sound kept getting louder and louder.

I grabbed the phone and called Emily.

"She's breathing real funny," I said not wanting to say that this was the same way my grandmother was breathing before she died. "She really doesn't sound good. Should I call nine-one-one?"

"No, don't call them," she said calmly. "Just give her some water."

I kept Emily on the phone while I rushed to the kitchen, filled a glass, then brought back the water. But when I tried to give a little to Ms. Neil, she still could hardly lift her head, and she wasn't swallowing.

"The water isn't working," I told Emily. "I'm gonna call her doctor."

"Okay, you can do that," Emily said. "But whatever you do, don't call the police."

"Okay," I said, wondering why she didn't want me to make the emergency call. What was going on?

But, I couldn't think about that too long. I hung up the phone and tried to give Ms. Neil some more water, but when she couldn't lift her head, I stopped. I didn't want her to choke.

Now, I was really scared. I didn't have any experience with this. All I'd done with my grandmother was keep her comfortable, sit with her, talk to her. Yes, I changed her diaper, and fed her, but I didn't have to do anything like this.

I put down the glass and picked up the phone again. I really wanted to talk to her doctor. But before I could make the call, all of a sudden, Ms. Neil sprang up in the bed and grabbed my arm with such a strong grip, I couldn't pull away.

"Stop!" I said.

Her eyes were wide open, almost bulging as she began to shake so hard. I don't know how I knew, but I was sure that she was dying.

"Oh, my God!" I yelled as I tried to peel her off of me.

But her grip was too strong. My heart was beating so hard it felt like it left my body. This woman was dying and she wouldn't let me go. I was freaking out!

One by one, I finally pried her fingers off of my arm, dropped the phone, and went screaming out the door. I ran to the end of the driveway, waving my hands in the air the whole time. I knew I probably looked crazy, but I needed to stop somebody, anybody!

"Help!" I yelled as cars rode right past me.

Finally, a guy in a black pickup truck slowed down and pulled over.

"What's wrong?"

"Please help me. I think she's dying! I think she's dying!" I could hardly breathe.

"Who?" he asked as he jumped out of his truck.

I couldn't speak, so I just pointed to the house. He ran inside and then, he followed me into the bedroom. Ms. Neil wasn't sitting up the way she was when I ran out. She was laying down and the man rushed to her side.

"She's dying!" he said. "Let me do CPR."

I pressed my back against the wall and watched as the man breathed into her mouth and then pumped her chest. But after he did these a few times, he stopped.

"She's dead," he said softly.

"Oh, my God." I grabbed the phone, and then ran out of the room. In the living room, I paced back and forth as I called my mother. She had barely answered the phone when I started screaming, "Mom, where you at?"

"I'm on my way. I'm on the island. What's wrong?"

"She's dead, Mama. She's dead." Tears were flowing from my eyes. "What to do? What to do?"

"Oh, my God. I'm on my way, Shicka! I'm almost there."

I looked back down the hall to Ms. Neil's bedroom, but I couldn't go back there. So, I rushed outside to wait for mother. Right now, I didn't even want to be in that house.

Within five minutes my mother pulled up. She jumped out of her car and hugged me.

"Are you all right?" she asked.

I nodded because I was trembling so much it was hard for me to speak.

"Okay," my mom said. "Let me go see her."

Slowly, I followed my mother into Ms. Neil's bedroom. The man was still there, and I was so grateful that he had stayed because without him, I didn't know what I would've done. He said to my mother, "I just called nine-one-one. They're on their way."

The whole time, I kept my eyes on the man because I was too afraid to look at Ms. Neil. But finally, I picked up enough courage to look at her.

Ms. Neil was laying in the bed like I'd left her. Her mouth was wide open and her tongue was hanging out. Her eyes were wide open, too, and had changed colors, from her normal gray to a greenish blue.

My mother walked over to the bed and with the tips of her fingers, she gently closed Ms. Neil's eyes. Then, she said, "The Lord is my shepherd, I shall not want."

I stood there as my mother said the entire 23rd Psalm and I wondered how could she do that? How could she stand there next to that dead woman? How could she touch her?

When my mother finished, the man who had helped me said, "I'm gonna leave now."

He walked out, and when my mother followed him, I ran out of there right behind her. My mother thanked the man, then let him out the door. When she came back in, I asked her, "Mama, you're not scared?"

"No, baby. She's dead and she's gone home."

I started shaking my head. "Mama, I can't do this work. I just can't. I don't want to see people die. I want people to live."

"I know, baby," my mother said. "I'll go outside and wait for the paramedics. Did you call Emily?"

"Oh, no," I said. "I forgot."

"Call her," my mother told me.

As my mother went outside, I called Emily. "Ms. Neil is gone," I told her the moment she answered the phone. "She's dead."

"Oh, wow," she said. "I'll be right there."

I hung up from her, but that question was still in my mind... why didn't Emily want me to call nine-one-one? And what would've happened if I had made that emergency call anyway? Would Ms. Neil still be alive?

For a long time, what happened with Ms. Neil had me scared of death. And for a long time, what happened kept me from answering the true call on my life.

I didn't want to do home health care anymore. Yes, I liked working with my grandmother, but I couldn't help people. I couldn't help anyone if they were going to die.

So when Ms. Neil died, I decided right then that I needed to find something else to do. I found something else, but it didn't keep me away from the calling on my life for too long. I couldn't run away from what God really wanted me to do.

CHAPTER 23

To me, Ms. Neil dying was a sign that I wasn't supposed to be doing home health care. I needed to be back in an office. Nobody died in an office building.

After looking through the newspaper for a couple of days, I found a job as an Intake Specialist at Rent-A-Party Center. My job was to take down the information of people who wanted to order supplies from us; anything from linen, to table skirting, to china—whatever people needed for their parties.

I had been there for only a few days when I realized that I really didn't know how to do this job. I'd always been smart and could usually figure out anything, but with this job, I had to do a lot of writing. And because I'd dropped out of school, my spelling wasn't the best, my grammar wasn't the best, and I felt like the manager was always watching over me, looking for my mistakes.

Plus, it wasn't such a good working environment. All the people who worked there were kind of uppity. They all had college degrees and the way they talked, using big words that I didn't understand, just made me feel like I didn't fit in. No matter what I did, I felt really uncomfortable in that place.

Because I was always a responsible person, I kept going to that job, day-after-day, always trying to do better. But it just kept getting worse and worse. I complained to my mom about it just about every day.

One day, when I went over to my mom's house, she sat me down and really talked to me.

"I know you don't like that job, Shicka. What you love is working with older people. You have a heart for them. When you were interacting with Grandma and even Ms. Neil, I could see it. You have something special. You were happy then."

"But Ms. Neil died!"

"And we knew she was gonna die. She was old and sick. But don't let what happened with Ms. Neil stop you. Because think about it, that little time that you did spend with her, you made her life worth living.

"Plus, Shicka," she continued, "You never experienced anyone dying before. Not in front of you like that. I pray that you'll never have to experience something like that again, but that's a part of it. But the truth is, home health care...that's what you need to be doing."

Sitting at my mother's kitchen table, I just let her words sink in before I finally said, "You know what, Mama, you're right."

Everything my mother said was right. I really wanted to go right then and find something in home health care. But, I'd have to wait just a little while because while I was having my own problems, my mother was having her problems, too.

Right when I started working at the rental party company, my mom told me that she wanted to move.

"I can't stay out here anymore, Shicka. All of this reminds me too much of Mama."

I understood. My mother and my grandmother had spent so much time together in that trailer and with everything that my grandmother had been through, there were too many memories for my mom there. And it didn't help that Gerald was nowhere to be found. So, my mother was spending a lot of time all the way out in Odum by herself.

My mother told me that she wanted to move back to Brunswick. "I need to go back home."

"Okay, well, I'm gonna find you a place, but you should come stay with me and Tre until we get you something."

So, she stayed with us for a couple of months and I did find my mom a place—over on Lee Street. My mother and I put our money together and got her that apartment, furnished it, and wouldn't you know—that's when Gerald started coming back around, though he never did stay long.

Every time I saw him, I got sick. I would lecture my mom, "He's not good for you. You really need to leave him this time. He wasn't even there for you when you needed him with Grandma, you were all by yourself taking care of her. It's just not fair."

But no matter what I said, I wasn't able to convince my mother. Not until she took a trip to Jacksonville because that's where Gerald said he was working. As it turned out, he was down in Jacksonville working all right. He was working and was down there messing around with some woman.

When my mother came back, she had finally made up her mind.

"Shashicka, you're right," she said. "I'm really tired of him. I'm done."

After all these years, I was so happy to hear that, but I had to wait and see if my mother was really going to do what she said.

It still took a couple of months, but finally one day when I went to see my mother, she said, "I'm ready now."

I had forgotten about our conversation, so I said, "You're ready to do what?"

"I'm ready to file for my divorce, and I will as soon as I get the money."

My mother had hardly finished when I said, "You don't have to wait. I got the money!"

I couldn't wait to leave my mother's house and get to the bank! I didn't have a whole lot in savings, but I got that six hundred dollars out and paid the lawyer. Like I said, I couldn't do it fast enough. This was the man who'd brought so much grief to my mother. Those childhood memories of her getting beaten were still in my mind. All I could think about was the hell that he'd taken us through.

A few days later, my mother filed the papers. To make sure the divorce went through quickly, she put an ad in the paper, making like she didn't know where Gerald was. Thirty days later, the divorce was final since 'she didn't know where he was' and he never responded to the notice in the paper. But that was fine with me...Gerald was gone! That was all I cared about. My prayer was that we would never see or hear from that man again!

CHAPTER 24

After I had that talk with my mother about what I really wanted to do, I stayed at the party center for just a few more months before I decided that I was going to pursue my dream. Helping the elderly, helping the sick and shut-in was truly my passion. I put what had happened with Ms. Neil out of my mind and decided I was going to give it one more try.

So, I put another ad in the newspaper and this time, I got a call from a woman on Sea Island. She needed twenty-four hour care as well because she was in her seventies and had just had both of her hips replaced. After speaking with her on the phone, I arranged to meet Mrs. Duggins at her home. I was surprised when she opened the door when I got there. I didn't know if she was able to move around, I didn't know if there was anyone else there with her. But she was alone.

"Follow me," was all she said after she opened the door and looked me up and down.

I followed her into her bedroom, and we talked in there.

"Well, let me tell you what I need," she said getting right to the point and not being too friendly. "I need twenty-four hour care."

"Yes, ma'am," I said, thinking that she had already told me this over the phone. I'd already called my mother and her friend who had worked with us with Ms. Neil.

"I need somebody to come in and be my maid."

Her maid? I thought that I would just be taking care of her. Maybe sitting with her, and making some of her meals.

She continued, "When you come in in the morning, I'll give you a list of things you need to do. Oh, I'll be using this." Then, she leaned over and picked up a huge cowbell. She shook it and it was so loud, it echoed against the walls, making it seem like the sound would never stop. "Whenever you hear this," she rang it again, "you need to be coming in here to see what I want."

My eyes opened wide. I couldn't believe she was talking to me like this.

She said, "I'm paying you guys and I already feel like I'm paying you too much money, but I need your help until I can get better. So, you're gonna come in here and do what I need you to do. You hear me?"

I nodded.

"I'm gonna get rid of my maid 'cause I don't need her anymore since you guys are gonna be the ones to clean."

She looked at me and had such a frown on her face, I could tell that she really didn't like me. Then she said, "Now, once I get better with my hips, I'm gonna get rid of you guys 'cause like I said, I'm already paying you too much and I won't need you anymore."

Wow! That was all I could think. I was telling myself that maybe I should just walk out of there, but the only thing was—

she was paying us very good money and I had already quit my job.

Plus, she had this beautiful house on Sea Island. It wasn't spooky like Ms. Neil's. This home had cost a lot of money, I could tell. And the furniture was beautiful. Every room looked like it came straight out of a magazine. I liked everything—except for Mrs. Duggins.

But I guessed that I didn't have to really like her. I just had to work for her.

The next morning when I walked into her house with the key she had given me, she called out to me, "Come here, gal!"

Gal? Mrs. Duggins knew my name. I'd told her. But that was the first time she called me, "Gal," and she continued to call me that for a whole year.

"You can start this morning by cutting the grass," she told me.

Really?

"I need you to make sure that my lawn always looks neat, Gal," she demanded.

"Okay," I said, wondering if working for her was going to work out. But I just kept thinking about the money.

Once I finished cutting the grass, I went back into the house, into her bedroom, and told her that I was finished.

"Already? I hope you did a good job," she said in a tone that sounded like she was angry. "Okay, well now, I want you to go up to the attic."

"To the attic? For what?"

"Go up there and lay out the rat traps."

"Rat traps?"

"Yes, I want you to lay them out every morning. That's the first thing you should do when you get here."

"I didn't think I'd be doing anything with rats."

"Well, you're the maid. You're supposed to do what I want you to do."

"No, Mrs. Duggins," I said, as calmly as I could. "We're your caregivers, not your maid."

She sucked her teeth and waved her hand in the air. "That's just a fancy word for maid."

All I could do was shake my head. I thought I'd be helping Mrs. Duggins with her cooking and cleaning, maybe going out and running errands for her. I didn't think I'd be doing anything with rats!

She added, "And when you catch the rats, then I want you to dig a hole in the backyard and bury them." She paused. "You got that, Gal?"

I couldn't believe this lady. But, I kept my mind on the money and went up to the attic, set the traps, and the prayed that I didn't see too many rats.

But every morning, I was back up in the attic. And when I found rats in the traps, I took them and buried them in the backyard like she wanted.

 After that I would do some of the things that I'd expected to do: I'd clean and cook for her. Mrs. Duggins worked me my entire shift. I never took a break, from seven in the morning until four in the afternoon. All day long, I listened to her ringing that cowbell, calling me gal, and never touching anything that I touched. When I brought her a cup of coffee, she wouldn't even touch the handle. She'd grab a napkin and then lift the cup as if she was afraid to touch anything that I put my hands on. Honestly, sometimes being with Mrs. Duggins felt like slavery.

But, I needed the money, and I needed the job. So, I stayed, did my work. And about a year after I started there, things changed with Mrs. Duggins. I guess because I worked well with her and did everything that she asked, she went from being like the mean ole stepmother to a fairy godmother. She was a fairy godmother who would teach me so much and who would eventually really change my life.

CHAPTER 25

I was shocked when one day, Mrs. Duggins called me into her bedroom and said, "You know what, Shicka, you really are a beautiful girl."

"Thank you," I said.

"Sit down," she said. "I want to talk to you."

I was waiting to see if she was upset about something since she had never asked me to sit in her room before. But she seemed to be fine. She said, "You know you're young. You have your whole life ahead of you. You don't want to be doing this for the rest of your life, do you?"

I shrugged because I didn't know what else to say.

She said, "You need to make sure you marry well. You need to marry someone like a doctor or lawyer. I want you to be with someone who's rich."

I almost laughed. *Really?* She must not have remembered that I was already married. I told her that. And Tre was far from a doctor or lawyer.

But, I didn't feel like explaining that to Mrs. Duggins. So, all I said was, "Okay." And then, I got up and went about my work.

The next day, Mrs. Duggins said, "You know what? I still want you to marry well, but I know that you're going to make something of yourself, too."

"I hope so," I said.

She asked, "What is it that you really want to do?"

At first, I hesitated, but then, I told Mrs. Duggins about my dream. "I really like what I'm doing and one day, I want to open up a home health care agency."

She nodded. "That's a really good business to get into," she said. "Because of the baby boomers. There're a lot of people getting old. And there are a lot of people like me."

Then I told her how I got interested in all of this. I told her a little about when I took care of my grandmother. "But, I don't know how to start a business. I don't know where to begin and I don't have any money."

"Well, you have to start first with money and what you need to do is you need to save money."

"That's really hard to do," I told her. In my head, I added up what I was making. I was only getting about five hundred dollars a week from Mrs. Duggins and then, after I paid my mother and the other lady, I only had about two hundred dollars for myself. There was no way I could save money on that. "I'm not making much," I told her as if she didn't know.

Mrs. Duggins said, "Everyone can save money. Like, when do you get a lump sum?"

"Of money?" I asked. I shook my head. "I don't have anyone sending me money in a lump sum. The only thing that I would have coming in would be at the beginning of the year when I file my taxes."

"Ding-dong!"

I frowned. "What does that mean?"

"There you go. Save your taxes 'cause you can't miss something that you never had."

I sat quietly for a moment, thinking about what she said. Inside my head, I was telling her all the things I had to do when I got my taxes—like pay all my backed up bills. I needed to use my tax refund to get caught up on everything that I couldn't pay with my regular paycheck. "I don't know, Mrs. Duggins," I said. "When I get that money, I need to use it."

"I understand," she said. "But you need to learn how to budget." She pointed to a table across her bedroom. "Bring me a piece of paper and a pen."

Right there, she sat me down and showed me how to add up all of my bills on one side and then all of the money I was earning on the other. And from there, every day, she taught me a little something about money. But even with all of her millions, Mrs. Duggins didn't give me anything—at least not anything that cost money. She gave me something more valuable—she gave me information, she gave me an education. And she taught me how to earn—and want to earn—everything that I got. I didn't know it then, but the information that I was getting from Mrs. Duggins would change my life in so many ways.

When I got my income tax a few months later, the Federal check was almost six thousand dollars. Then, the State check was another seven hundred and something dollars.

So with almost seven thousand dollars, I paid off a few bills, the main ones, and then I made payment arrangements with the companies that I could. After I took care of what I had to, I had a little over three thousand left.

But once I had that money, I wasn't sure what I was supposed to do next. Yes, I had three thousand dollars to go toward my business, but what was I supposed to do with that money? What were the next steps?

For days, I wondered, and I couldn't come up with anything. So one day, while standing at Mrs. Duggins stove, I opened my mouth and prayed, "God, please help me. I really want to have a home health care business, but I need you to help me create this vision. Please guide my footsteps because I don't even know what to do."

It was as if God was right there in the kitchen with me. For the second time in my life, I heard God as if he was standing next to me. "Shashicka," I heard Him say, "you know what it is you want to do. You have to take the proper steps."

The proper steps. I let God's words settle in me and after I took Mrs. Duggins her lunch, I grabbed the phone book that she had in the kitchen. The first thing that I had to do was what every business owner needed to do—I had to get a license. So, I called the City of Brunswick and when the lady answered, I told her what I needed.

"I need to find out how to get licensed to do home health care."

I heard tapping on her computer keys, and then she said, "Well, ma'am, we don't issue licenses for that. You have to go through the State. All you have to do is apply with the State."

The State? Wow! My heart felt like it fell all the way to the floor. I was just getting started and already, I was discouraged. How was I going to apply with the State? I lived in Brunswick and the furthest away I'd ever been was Jacksonville and Miami. The State—wherever that was—seemed so far away.

All of this money that I had saved and all of the hope that I had just seemed to be falling away. I hung up the phone not quite sure what I was going to do.

For weeks after talking to that lady, I was worried and borderline depressed because I didn't even know how I was going to accomplish the first step. I found out that 'the State' was in Atlanta. Forget about steps two, three, and four...I couldn't even get past step one. How was I going to get to Atlanta?

It was my mom who finally helped me break through. One day when she came to take over her shift with Mrs. Duggins, she looked at me and said, "Shicka, what's wrong? I can tell for the past couple of weeks that something's bothering you."

I nodded. "I'm ready to open up my business and I really want to do it, but the lady on the phone told me that I have to apply with the State. And after I did some research I found out that it's way in Atlanta."

"Way in Atlanta?" my mother said like she was confused. "Atlanta is right up the road. It's just four hours away."

"Just four hours?"

"Yeah."

Okay, four hours didn't seem too far when I had driven five hours to Miami. Still, it seemed scary to me. "But...I've never been there before."

My mother shook her head and looked me straight in the eye. "Shicka, the only way you're going to get what you want is if you go out there and grab it. If you really want it, you'll get it. You'll do whatever it takes to get it. You'll find a way to deal with the people in Atlanta."

"Thank you, Mama," I said as I hugged her. Then, I got into my car feeling better than I had in weeks. Just those few little words from my mother had motivated me so much. Because of my mother, I was on my way to pursuing my dream! I was going to do what she said. I was going to get what I wanted. I was going to grab my dream.

CHAPTER 26

As soon as I got to my house, I picked up the phone and called the State office in Atlanta. This time, the lady knew exactly what I needed.

"We do issue licenses here," she told me. "There's a process you have to go through. First you have to apply on the Internet. Just fill out the form, and then, we'll send you the class dates."

"Class dates?"

"Yes, you have to take classes."

"Where are the classes?"

"Right here in Atlanta."

Oh, my God! Here I go again. If I had to go to Atlanta to take classes, this would never work. How long were the classes and where would I stay?

Just as I was thinking that, the lady said, "Now, you do have to have a high school diploma, right?"

That just made everything worse. I never went back to school after I had LaMiracle, so what was I going to do now? But before

I could get too down about it, I thought about what my mother said. Yes, I really did want this. So, that meant that I was going to have to do whatever it would take!

That's what I did.

I found out where to take GED classes and I started right away. It was going to take me some years to finish since I'd dropped out of school when I was fourteen. But even though it was going to be a long road, I was determined to do it.

So every day, I went to work from seven to four and then right after that, I would go to school. It was a lot and it was hard. Going to work, going to school, and still taking care of my family, my children.

From the beginning, I told Tre what I was doing. But my husband was so into the streets then that he wasn't interested in what I had going on. I cannot tell you how bad that made me feel. What I was trying to do, took a lot, and it was for our future. I needed that support from my husband. But, thank God for my mother.

My mom just kept pushing me over and over. Telling me, "Shicka, you can do it! You can do it!"

My mother wasn't the only one supporting me. I had several women who helped me, especially women who helped me with LaMiracle and Xavier. Besides my mom who was always there to help with my kids in any way I needed, I had a neighbor, Ayesha, who helped out when she could.

But the biggest help was my dad's girlfriend, LaTasha Smith. I hadn't known LaTasha very long. My father brought her by the house one day because he wanted to introduce us to his new girlfriend.

My father walked into our house all proud and everything. "This is LaTasha," he said. And then, he added, "She's nineteen."

Wow! Just nineteen? She was way too young for him, and I began to worry about her. Why was she with someone that old? Did LaTasha know about my father and his drug use? Or was she using drugs with him?

But I didn't ask either one of them anything. I just invited them in and we sat and talked. I found out that she was staying at the hotel with my father, and she didn't seem like she was on any kind of drugs.

The two of them would come over to our place from time to time and LaTasha seemed like a nice enough girl. Then one night, I found out how nice...and innocent she really was.

It was about two o'clock in the morning when my cell phone rang. My eyes were hardly open when I answered the phone.

"Shicka," a woman's voice said my name. Whoever it was on the other end was crying.

"Yeah."

"This is LaTasha!"

It took me a moment to get my bearings. "Tasha, what's wrong?"

"Shicka, your father's smoking crack!" she said as if she was telling me something I didn't know.

I frowned. Okay, she'd been with my father for a while and she was just finding this out? "Tasha, you didn't know he was on crack?"

"No! And now I feel so uncomfortable 'cause I've never been around anyone using drugs like that."

Really? I thought to myself. But what I said was, "Why don't you just go home?"

She paused for a moment. "I don't have any place to go."

Wow! All kinds of memories rushed back to me. All the memories of when I was a teenager and on my own. My heart hurt for her. "Well, where's your mom?"

"My mom put me out."

It was because the same thing had happened to me that I said, "I tell you what, I'll come and get you. You can spend the night here and then we'll figure something out in the morning."

"Thank you," she said.

I could hear the gratitude in her voice. I rolled out of the bed and drove over to the hotel where my father was staying. LaTasha was waiting for me outside. She was still crying and really upset and I could tell that she had been telling me the truth—she really hadn't ever been around drugs like this before—not with the way she was acting.

When we got back to my house, we didn't go to bed right away. She was so upset that I didn't want to leave her alone. So, we just sat in the living room and talked. I found out that night all about LaTasha Smith. To that point, I didn't know a thing about her, except that she was my dad's nineteen-year-old girlfriend. But now that she was going to be here, I wanted to know who I had spending the night in my house.

I said, "You know, you really don't want to be with someone who's using drugs like that."

Her tears were still falling when she said, "I really don't want to be with your dad, but when he saw me on the street and found out that I didn't have a place to stay, he took me in. That's how I ended up being with him."

In that instant, I had more memories: the time I met that guy on the road and ended up sleeping with him just so I could have enough money to get my first apartment. LaTasha wasn't that different from me. She was just doing what I did—whatever she had to do so that she could get by.

She told me about her mom and how abusive her mom had been to her.

"I was getting an SSI check because of my father," Tasha told me. "But my mom would take my money and just beat on me. All the time."

Listening to her stories made me feel even more sorry for her. Finally, we went to sleep, but the next morning, I told her that I had to go to work.

"So, you're gonna have to leave or do something," I said. I wasn't going to leave someone I didn't know in my house.

"I have an idea," she said. "You don't have to take the kids to daycare. I can take care of them and help you out around here."

LaTasha seemed like a nice girl, but I didn't know her. And I wasn't going to leave anyone I didn't know around my kids.

"No, I'm gonna take the kids to daycare, so you're gonna have to find something else to do and then, when I get off, you can come back."

That's what she did. LaTasha left the house with us and I don't know what she did during the day, but then, she came back over when I got home. She did that every day for a whole week. She'd leave with me in the morning and come back at night.

Every night we talked more and more and I got more comfortable with her. The more I got to know her, the more I liked her, the more I wanted to help. She was really a good girl who was in a world of trouble and it made sense that we could help each other.

So, she ended up moving in with me and things got even better! LaTasha did everything with the kids: she'd get them ready for school, walk them to the bus stop, and in the afternoon, she'd be there to meet them after school.

So while Tre was running the streets, coming in at two and three o'clock in the morning, with the help of a few women,

I was able to stay focused on what I had to do. I could keep studying so that I could get my GED.

It took three months, but I did it. Once I had my GED in my hand, I called the Atlanta office back and told the woman that I was ready for the next steps.

"Great," she told me. "We have your application that you submitted on-line and I'll send you a schedule for the class dates. You are ready to take the classes in Atlanta, right?"

"Yes, ma'am. Whatever I need to do, I'm ready."

"Okay," she said. "I'll get this in the mail to you."

A few days later, when I received the packet of information, I was so excited. I was jumping up and down like I already had my license. Of course, I didn't, but I was so on my way to pursuing my dreams and my goals and my visions.

The next classes were two months away and I told Tre that we were going to Atlanta.

"Okay," he said, nonchalantly. "Whatever. I'll see it whenever you get it." He shrugged his shoulders and dismissed me.

It hurt that I didn't have the support of my husband. He didn't encourage me at all—not even a little bit. Tre was still in the streets and I had no idea what he was doing. I was still getting calls from women, telling me that they were messing with my husband, that they were going to take him away, all of that. There was so much negative stuff going on at that time, but I did everything that I could to focus on the positive. In fact, the more negative that came at me, the harder I would strive. It was like I had something to prove to the world—like no one was going to stop me. I wasn't going to allow the devil to come at me in any way. I wasn't going to let the devil use Tre, or other women, or anything.

But the closer I came to my goals, the enemy seemed to come at me even harder. Until one day, the devil tried to take my dreams away completely. The devil tried to destroy me, once again using Tre. But this time, it wasn't another woman.

This time, it was jail. And Tre was going away for a long, long time.

CHAPTER 27

Just weeks before I was supposed to leave for Atlanta, Tre got caught hustling and I was shocked when he called me from jail.

"Shicka, I love you. I really love you, but there's something I have to tell you."

My heart was pounding when I said, "What?" Was he getting ready to tell me that he was leaving me again?

"I've been arrested and this time, I'm going away for a long time."

"Well, what did you do? What about bail?"

"I can't get none of that without a lawyer. But I don't have any money, so I know I won't get out and it'll be a long time before I'm out again."

I couldn't believe he didn't have any money. All of the time Tre spent in the streets, doing God knows what, Tre should've had a lot of money.

He said, "Just know that I love you and please take care of the kids."

"Okay," I said. My head was spinning with all kinds of thoughts. How long was he going to be gone? What were we going to do? Even though Tre stayed in the streets, he did bring home money when I needed it.

"I'm really sorry for this and the way I've been treating you," Tre said. "I'm really, really sorry for letting you down. Just remember that I love you, okay?"

When he hung up, all I could do was sit on the edge of the bed and cry. Even though Tre had not been supportive and had been bringing all kinds of negativity into my life, he was still my husband and I really believed in that. I know other women may have reacted differently, but I'm just a person who is so dedicated to my family; everyone, my husband, my children, my mom.

I had to do something. I couldn't leave my husband in jail like that. Not only did I not want him to be in there, but I was getting ready to take those classes in Atlanta. I wanted, I needed Tre to be with me.

But when I called around for lawyers, the best price I could get was an attorney who wanted five thousand dollars. I had three thousand dollars that I had saved, but that was for my business. I needed that money to keep my dream alive and there was no way I was going to use it. I had to find money for Tre some other way.

I called up a friend of Tre's and told him that I needed help.

"Okay, I'll come over," Philly told me.

But when he got there and I told him that I needed five thousand dollars to get a lawyer to help Tre, he told me that he didn't have any money.

"But, I got this." He pulled a plastic bag that looked like it was filled with powder.

I sat there looking at the bag of drugs. "What am I supposed to do with this?"

"Just make it work," he said. "This is what I can give you."

I thought about it for a moment, but only for a moment. There was no way I could do it. Drugs was against everything that I believed. I had seen too many people go down because of drugs...especially my father. I wanted my husband out of jail badly, but I wasn't going to do it this way.

Finally, I shook my head. "No, Philly, I can't do it."

"You sure? 'Cause this is what I got and it will get you what you need."

This time, I didn't even hesitate. "No, I'm not going to do it."

He shrugged and I walked Philly to the door. "Call me if you change your mind," he said. "I'm here for you and my boy."

I closed the door and right away tears came to my eyes because I knew what I had to do. I didn't want to do it, but in my heart, Tre was worth more than any dream. I had to take care of my family first. The next day, I went to the bank and withdrew the three thousand dollars I had saved for my business. It wasn't the five thousand that the attorney asked for, but I figured I'd be able to find someone who would take Tre's case for the three thousand.

It was a hard thing to do, but like I said, I truly loved my husband. Tre needed a lawyer, and using my "dream money" was the only way I could help him. Plus, deep down in my heart I knew that if the tables were reversed, Tre would have been there for me. He would have done whatever he could to raise the money to get me out of jail. Because Tre always came through at times like that. Just like he'd done with my grandmother.

Philly helped me to find an attorney who took the three thousand dollars and he got Tre a bond. Tre was shocked when he was let out and when he came home, I told him what I'd done.

"All of the money came from your savings for your business?"

I nodded.

"Wow. Thank you. And, I promise you. Whatever you need me to help you with, I'm going to be there for you."

I was relieved that Tre was home and now, I was excited, too. My husband was going to help me. I didn't have any money, so I worked double shifts with Mrs. Duggins so that Tre and I would at least have money to get to Atlanta and stay in an inexpensive hotel. I had the money all figured out—thanks to Mrs. Duggins who'd taught me how to really plan.

So once again, I was focused on Atlanta and Tre was just as excited as I was. I may not have had the money that I had before, but I knew for sure that I was on my way to making all of my dreams come true.

CHAPTER 28

Throughout my life, my mother has always been there. Except for that time when I was fifteen and I didn't want her to marry Gerald, she has always been by my side. That's why one of the things I loved to do was hang out with my mother and just talk.

One day, when we were in the car together, my mother brought Gerald up out of the blue.

"You know, Shicka, Gerald took me through so much."

I had always wondered how she really felt about Gerald. She'd spent so much time defending him. "Yes, he did. He took all of us through a lot. I even feel like he took my childhood away from me." I shook my head. "You don't know what it was like to see your mom getting beat and not being able to do anything. Basically, he put us through hell."

My mother nodded and I could tell by the look in her eyes that she was sad and had so many regrets, especially for her children.

"He's gonna pay for it, Mom," I said, wanting her to feel better. "I just know it. He's gonna pay for it really soon. Just watch. Watch what I tell you."

All my mother did was nod, but her eyes were still filled with all kind of sadness. I hated that she felt bad when it was all Gerald's fault. But what I told my mom was the truth. I knew he was going to pay one day because no one could do what he'd done and get away with it for too long.

"And anyway, you don't need to be thinking about Gerald. You have Brian now," I said referring to the new guy that my mother had met.

Eight months after my mother's divorce was final, she had started dating Brian Jackson. The first time my mother brought him around, I knew he was a really good fellow. He seemed to treat my mother real nice and I could tell he was really into her.

But then, not long after that, I began to think that he was just another Gerald.

One day, I was driving through my neighborhood and I saw Brian's car. At first, I smiled, but then, I saw Brian. He was leaning on the hood of his car....and he was hugging...a woman....a white woman!

I had to blink a couple of times to make sure that I was really seeing what I was seeing. I pulled my car over, jumped out of the car, ready to beat Brian down.

"You were just with my Mama," I yelled at him. "What's going on with this here?"

"Your mama?" the woman asked before Brian could even answer me.

"Yeah, he's messing with my mama!"

"Well, I don't know who your mama is, but this is my man," the white lady said with major attitude.

"No, he's not," I shouted. "I'm gonna show you something." I pulled out my phone, called my mom, told her where I was and what I'd seen, and in less than ten minutes, she was there.

Her tires screeched across the asphalt as she sped up to the front of the house. She jumped out of the car, just like I'd done.

"Oh, you messing around now, huh?"

Brian held up his hands and just like the woman did to me, she started speaking before Brian.

"I don't know who you are," the woman said, "but this is my man."

"You know what? I'm not gonna deal with this," my mom said, getting back in her car. "I've been through this too much. I'm not going through it again."

I felt so bad because I'd thought Brian was one of the good guys. But I guess he wasn't.

My mom left him alone for a while. I guess she'd had enough with my father and she'd certainly had enough with Gerald.

But just a few months later, Brian came around to my mother. "It's over between me and her 'cause you're the one I want. I really want you, Darlene. You're who I want to be with."

"That's what you say, but I care more about what you do. I can't do this," my mother told him. "I'm not going through this again. Either you're going to be with me or her. You make the choice."

"I told you. I already made my choice. You're the one I want."

A few weeks after that, Brian moved in with my mom and I knew then that Brian was the one. I knew he would be the love of her life.

She had finally found love, so I didn't want her thinking about Gerald. I didn't want her feeling sorry about her time with that man. And I really didn't want her to feel bad about me, David and Jaime. We had made it. We were all fine.

When I pulled up in front of my mother's house, I asked her if she was okay.

"Yeah," she said. "I don't know why I started thinking about Gerald."

"Well, you don't need to think about him anymore. Just get him out of your mind, okay?"

She nodded, and I hugged her goodbye before I drove off, but all night, I kept thinking about how I was sorry that my mother felt bad. I knew that she had done the best that she could. At the time, she didn't think that she could do any better than Gerald, so that's why she stayed. I just hoped that she would be able to forgive herself one day.

The next morning, I received the most shocking phone call of my life.

"Shicka!"

"Yeah, who's this?"

"It's FaLinda."

FaLinda? Why was Gerald's sister calling me. It wasn't like we were friends or anything.

"Where's your mom? I'm trying to get in contact with your mom," FaLinda said, sounding like she was crying.

"My mom's at work. What's going on?"

"Shicka, Gerald's dead!" she said. "He got killed last night."

I shot up in my bed, hardly believing what I'd heard. I was so shocked I couldn't say anything.

"He's dead, Shicka. My brother is dead!" Then, she went on to tell me what happened. How Gerald was in Jacksonville, and someone tried to rob him. He'd tried to get away, he ran. But the guy shot him five times in the back.

I still couldn't say anything. All I could think about was what I'd told my mom yesterday.

He's gonna pay for it, Mom. I just know it. He's gonna pay for it really soon. Just watch. Watch what I tell you.

Oh, my God! Had I spoken this into existence?

"Okay," I said, finally able to get that word out. "I'll let my mom know."

My mother was just as shocked as I was, but she was sad also. One thing though, my mother never said anything to me about the conversation we'd had just the day before. She never mentioned how I had just about predicted Gerald's death. My mom went to Gerald's funeral, even though Brian didn't want her to go.

"I have to pay my respects," she explained to me and Brian.

I didn't go. I couldn't go. I didn't respect Gerald, not in any way. There was that time, when I got married where I'd tried to make peace with him, but that was only for my mother and it didn't last long. Not when he couldn't even be there to help my mother with her mother, not when he was in Jacksonville with that other woman, not when for years and years he'd taken my mom through hell.

I had given Gerald so many chances and I was done with all the chances. I didn't even have it in me to give him a chance at his funeral.

I was just done! At this point, all I could do was say that I hoped God blessed his soul.

CHAPTER 29

My focus in life was completely on my business and getting to Atlanta for these classes. I was working as hard as I could with Mrs. Duggins, trying to earn enough money to cover me and Tre for a week in Atlanta.

Me and Tre....even though Tre had promised that things would be better once he got out of jail, that only lasted about two weeks. He was right back in the streets. I really was devastated by that, but I still wasn't going to let Tre stop me. I was going to Atlanta, even if that meant going by myself. But then, when I said that I was leaving, Tre surprised me when he told me that he was still going with me.

"I told you I was going and I'm a man of my word. I'm going with you."

Having Tre with me meant a lot. So, I was happy once again when I packed up the kids to be with my mother and then Tre and I took the trip to Atlanta.

When we got there, I couldn't believe the state building where the classes were held. There had to be at least thirty floors in the building; it was the tallest building that I'd ever seen. We stayed at the Best Western downtown and I took the classes every day from 8 to 4.

The first time we went, we were there for a week. I took the classes, then we came back home to wait for the next classes to begin. I went back and forth to Atlanta about six times and every time, Tre went with me. For the first time in our marriage, Tre was always there for me.

It took me three months to finish all the classes, but I'd done it successfully. The next step was that I had to write my Policies and Procedures so that I could present my manual to the State.

Once again, like all the other steps, I panicked. I'd made it through the classes, but how was I supposed to write a manual? They'd given us a guide, but the guide didn't really help me that much. It was confusing, I didn't understand it at all. And even with the guide, I still had to come up with a lot of things, and I had to put it all in my own words.

How was I supposed to do this without any business knowledge, without any business classes? How was I supposed to do this not knowing at all what I was doing? But after getting my GED, and taking those classes, I wasn't about to give up now.

It took me about two weeks to pull it all together, to read the manual and write my procedures. When I was done, I called and made an appointment to return to Atlanta to present my Policies and Procedures to the State.

I was nervous when the day finally came, but in a way I was confident, too. Not only had I worked hard on the Policies and Procedures, but I'd held onto this dream for all of these years. I didn't have the money that I thought I would have since I'd used that for Tre, but I'd done everything else. All of this was going to pay off. I could feel it in my bones.

The morning of my appointment, Tre dropped me off, gave me a kiss, then I went inside. I found the office that the lady had told me to go to. It was a conference room really, that didn't have much furniture. All it had was a long conference table and chairs.

A white lady sat at the head of the table.

"Hello," I said when I entered the room.

All she did was nod and then made a motion for me to take the chair next to her.

Even though I was confident, I was nervous, especially looking at this woman. She didn't smile, in fact, she frowned the whole time.

"Those are your Policies and Procedures?" she kind of grunted.

"Yes, Ma'am," I said.

She took the pages from me and I sat down across from her at the table. I watched her as she looked over every page that I'd written, waiting the whole time for her to say something.

She never said anything. She never smiled. She just kept reading.

The room was just so quiet and as more time passed, I became even more nervous. I sat back in the chair and actually crossed my fingers. My prayer was that when this lady finished and I left the building, I would finally have the license that I needed to pursue my dream.

After about thirty minutes, the lady finally looked up. Without a smile or anything, she said, "Ma'am, you need to do this over."

"What?" I just knew that I hadn't heard her correctly.

"This doesn't make any sense!" she said to me as if she was disgusted. "This is all wrong."

I took the papers from her, stood up, then rushed out of the building. I was so grateful that I was able to hold my tears back until I was outside. Then, I cried.

In my mind, I went over everything that I had done, all the time I'd put in, all the struggles I had to get to this point. Why in the world was this happening now?

When I slid back into the car, Tre took one look at me. "What's wrong?"

"I didn't get it," I cried.

"That's okay," he said, trying to console me. "You'll get it the next time."

But I'm the kind of person that if I don't get something right the first time, it weighs heavy on me. I felt like such a failure.

The whole ride home, I cried and by the time we got back to Brunswick, I'd made up my mind I was just going to be done with it. I wasn't going to try again. I'd already given my best. What more was there to do after your best?

The first thing I did when I got home was call my mother. She answered the phone, so excited.

"Did you get it? Did you get it?" she asked.

That almost brought the tears back. "No, I didn't," I told her.

"Well that's okay, Shicka. Just try again."

"No, I'm not gonna try no more," I said. "I did everything that I could. I don't understand. I don't even know how to write these policies."

"Just do it again, Shicka. You can't give up now. Just do it again."

My mother said that so much that by the time I hung up, she'd convinced me. There was no way that I could give up. I had to try again.

So, I started studying everything that I could and every chance that I had. I would study at work while I was at Mrs. Duggins' house. Then, I would come home and study for hours. I didn't do anything except study from sunrise to sunset. Thank

God that LaTasha was still there helping me with Miracle and Xavier so that I could really concentrate.

I figured out where I'd made mistakes in my proposal and I fixed all of those. I worked on it until I was sure it was perfect.

When I was ready, I called the State for another appointment and they gave me one right away for the next week.

I was super-excited, even more this time than last time. To be able to get an appointment so quickly had to be a sign. This time, I would have that license, for sure.

The next week, Tre and I drove back up to Atlanta and when I walked into the office, there was the same lady.

"Hello," I said to her.

Like the last time, she didn't say anything. She just scowled at me as I handed her my new revised Policies and Procedures.

She nodded and I sat down in front of her. Just like before, she didn't say a word as she looked over what I'd written. And just like before, the room was quiet. About thirty minutes later, she looked up at me and I looked at her.

"This is worse than the first time!"

I couldn't believe she was saying this.

She said, "This is way worse than the first time. What you had before, you should have kept some of that."

It took me a couple of moments to get any words to come out. "You mean to tell me that I don't have it?"

"No, ma'am," she said, shaking her head. "I will not give you a license. You think I'm going to give you a license to start a business, a government-sanctioned business, and you got this mess on here?" She shook her head even harder now. "This is crap," she said as she almost threw the papers at me.

Tears raced down my face. How could this be happening again? Slowly, I took the papers from the lady, turned around and walked out the door. I was already crying when I got back in the car with Tre.

"Really?" he said without me saying a word.

I nodded. "I don't know what I'm doing wrong, but the lady said that this was crap."

Tre shook his head like he felt sorry for me. "I don't know, I just don't know. Is it that hard?"

"It's very hard!" I snapped. "But I studied and I just don't know what I'm doing wrong."

Just like the last time when I got home, I talked to my mom. But this time, her words were a little different.

"Shicka, the only thing I'm going to say is get off this phone and get on your knees. You need to ask God to help you."

Then, she hung up. That was it. That's all she had for me this time.

For a couple of minutes, I thought about what my mother had just told me to do, but I didn't pray. I couldn't pray. I couldn't even get down on my knees with the way I felt...I was so discouraged. It felt like my world was coming to an end because this was something that I'd worked so hard for and it seemed like I would never, ever get it.

But the whole night, I heard my mother's words in my head. "Shicka, get on your knees."

Her words ministered to me that night. And then the next day, and the next day. I began to hear my mother's words more and more and finally, I did it. About a week after I got back from Atlanta, I got on my knees and prayed. I prayed to God for His help and His guidance and His favor and His wisdom. When I got up, I had a new determination.

I told myself that I wasn't about to give up. I could do it. I began to tell myself that it was so easy.

Once again, I got straight into the books. I read and studied. But this time, I prayed also. When I read something that I didn't understand, I prayed for God to guide me.

"Please, show me the way, Lord."

And every time, God would take me right to everything that I needed.

This time, a month passed and I called the State again. For the third time. They needed to know that I was ready to come back.

The lady on the phone warned me, "Shashicka, if you don't pass this time, if you don't get those policies and procedures right, it will be two years before you can apply again."

"That's fine," I told her, not scared at all by her words. "I'm ready."

This time, on the entire ride to Atlanta, as Tre drove, I prayed.

"Lord, Jesus, please help me. God you know how bad I need this. I want to be able to help not only myself, but other people in the process." I just kept praying and praying, the same words over and over again.

When I got to the building, it was the same thing. The same room. The same lady.

She looked up at me. "Oh, you're back, huh? I wasn't looking for you for another three or four months, but you're back here in a month?" She shook her head. "That's impossible. I bet you don't have them right," she said without even looking at what I'd done. It was like she wasn't going to even give me a chance.

I didn't say a word; I just stood my ground.

"All right, I'll look at them," she said as she held out her hand. "I'll be glad to tell you that you don't have them right again, and this time, I won't have to see you for another two years."

If she thought she was intimidating me, she wasn't. I said, "You know what? God got me."

She frowned. "God got you?"

"Yes, ma'am. God got me. So, even if I don't get my license, even if this is still all wrong, God is still going to have me."

This time when I sat down in front of her, I prayed. She kept looking over my papers, grunting and shaking her head. It didn't matter, I still prayed.

"Lord, in your name," I prayed out loud. Tears were already falling out of my eyes, but I still prayed. "In your name, Jesus."

The more I called on Jesus, the more she grunted like everything that she was reading was wrong.

Finally she looked up and said, "You must really want this license."

"Yes, ma'am. I want this license with everything in my soul."

She looked at me. "Baby, I'm gonna tell you something." She paused. "I don't know how you did it, but you're approved!"

I jumped up and yelled. "I'll tell you how I did it. God did it!" I shouted. "Thank you, Jesus!"

I praised God in that building. I praised Him so hard, people started walking out of the other offices coming to see what was happening.

"What's going on?" people asked as they peeked into the conference room.

But, I couldn't answer none of them. All I could say was, "Thank you, Jesus!" I was screaming my praise. I fell to my knees, continuing my praise and worship right there on the floor in the middle of the office in the state office building.

Right there, I made promises to God, thanking Him and letting Him know that I was going to help people. Finally, I was able to stand up and talk to the people when they asked what was going on.

"I'm just giving God the praise," I said to the men and women who had filled the office watching me. "'Cause if it wasn't for Him, none of this would be possible. I remember walking in this building plenty of days and I didn't have God on my mind. But this time, I had God on my mind and on my heart. And I got this license."

This time when I got in the car to head back to Brunswick, I was crying, but for a different reason. The ride back to Brunswick was the best car ride I'd ever had in my life. I had my license in my hand.

And not only that, the lady told me that I was the first African American and the youngest applicant to have a license in the State of Georgia for home health care.

I was only twenty one years old!

I had always known God, He was always a part of my life. But what I'd done this time was keep God at the center of my life as I went for my license. And this just proved something that I wanted to shout to the world: if you really want something and you go after it with God, anything is possible.

That's where I had made the mistake before. The two previous times, I had worked hard, but I'd forgotten about God. I'd been thinking that I could do it by myself.

But it took God to go in there with me, to help me get what I needed! This was proof that without God, I could do nothing! But with Him, I could do it all!

CHAPTER 30

I was floating on Cloud Nine the whole ride back to Brunswick and I was still walking on that cloud when I went to work the next day. I couldn't wait to bust into Mrs. Duggins house and rush into her bedroom.

"Mrs. Duggins, I got my license!"

Calmly, she looked up at me. "Oh, you do, huh?"

"Yes, ma'am."

"Well, what you gonna do now?"

I didn't say anything at first. But then, I said, "I don't know, Mrs. Duggins. I guess I'm just gonna stay here for now."

She just shook her head.

I did stay there with Mrs. Duggins. For another month. And then another month, and then a third month. Three months had gone by and I was sitting there with that license that I had worked so hard for in my hand. But, I hadn't done anything else. I hadn't taken the next steps.

The truth was, I was afraid. I was afraid to get out there on my own.

But, I kept praying and praying and the time finally came one day when my mother walked through the door. It was just an ordinary day. My mother came to relieve me from my shift. She said hello, hugged me and then asked what I was doing.

But this time, my answer to her was different from all the other days. This time, I said, "Mom, I got to go. My time is up. God has blessed me with this license and I've got to do this so that I won't let Him down. I promised Him that I was gonna help other people, so I've got to do this.

"I'm gonna help people get jobs, I'm gonna help people who thought that they would never be able to make it. Nobody helped me, but I'm not gonna do people like that. So when people come to me for jobs, I'm gonna let them know that I got them. I'm gonna give them opportunities. So Mama, I got to go. My time is up."

My mother looked at me with tears in her eyes. "So what are we going to do about Mrs. Duggins?"

"You can do it," I told my mother. "You can handle it, you're just gonna have to take over 'cause I'm not supposed to be here. It's time for me to go and get on my own."

My mother smiled and hugged me. "Well, you need to go in there and let Mrs. Duggins know what you're gonna do."

Even though she was the one who'd encouraged me, talking to Mrs. Duggins about leaving was going to be hard. She and I had become so close. What started out as what I thought was a racist relationship had turned into almost a mother and daughter closeness. Mrs. Duggins really had a heart for me and I had a heart for her.

Slowly, I walked into her room and stood at the door for a moment. Mrs. Duggins was sitting in her chair, looking over some papers. Then, she looked up with a smile on her face.

"Mrs. Duggins, I need to talk to you."

The frown came right onto her face and her tone was sharp. But she didn't fool me anymore. "What do you want to talk to me about?" she asked, sounding like she didn't have time for me. "Can't you see that I'm busy?"

"Well, this is really important," I said. I took a deep breath and continued, "I want you to know that my time is up."

"What do you mean your time is up?"

"My time is up. I need to go ahead and start doing what I told you I wanted to do. I want to start pursuing my dreams and open up this home care agency."

"Does that mean you're not going to work for me anymore?" She didn't give me a chance to answer. "You can still do that and work for me."

I shook my head. "No, I can't. That's what I've been trying to do. I've stayed here, but I'm not getting anywhere. I need to be out so that I can market my company."

Right away, sadness washed all over her face. It took her a couple of moments to speak. "I'm gonna miss you," she said in the softest voice that she had ever used with me.

"I'm gonna miss you, too."

She tilted her head to the side. "I know I taught you all that stuff and I wanted you to go after your dreams, but I really don't want you to go."

"I know," I said. "I don't want to leave, but...."

She said, "Can I pay you more to stay?"

"This isn't about the money. This is about me doing what I know God has called me to do. But, I promise you," I said as I moved closer to her, "I will come and see you as much as I can. And you know my mom will take care of you." When I stood in front of her, I saw the tears in her eyes and it broke my heart.

I started crying, too. This woman who started out calling me, "Gal," really cared about me. Mrs. Duggins always pretended to be so hard and so tough, but this woman had this heart of gold.

She reached out her arms and I stood there for a moment. It looked like she wanted me to hug her, but I knew that couldn't be it. As close as we'd become, Mrs. Duggins wasn't into that kind of affection. She didn't want anyone touching her, she wanted no physical contact whatsoever.

"You want me to give you a hug?" I asked just to be sure.

She nodded. "Yeah."

When she held me, I couldn't believe how tight her grasp was. And she held me as the seconds went by. "I'm gonna miss you," she whispered to me again. "But, I know you have to go."

She stepped back from me. "So you're really ready to do this."

"Yes, ma'am."

"How much money you got?"

I paused for a moment. I hadn't been able to save as much with all the trips back and forth to Atlanta and I really didn't want to tell her what I had. i didn't want to explain how I'd used most of it for Tre. "I have seven hundred dollars."

She frowned. "Doesn't sound like much."

"It's not," I said. "But I know it's time."

This time, she nodded. "I know that, too. Just make sure you call me and come by."

When I walked out of her bedroom, I didn't look back. When I walked out of her house, I didn't look back. I kept my eyes forward the whole time. I kept my eye on my prize.

The next morning was the first time in two years that I didn't go to Mrs. Duggins. Instead, I went out looking at office space. One of the first buildings I looked at was on Grant Street. The office was in an alley, right across the street from The Red Carpet Lounge—one of Brunswick's strip clubs.

It wasn't much of anything. In fact, the office was about the size of a walk-in closet. The office was connected to another office that was in the back and the second office was even smaller. The entire office was about the size of a bedroom and the office needed some work—the paint on the walls was chipping and the floors were scuffed up. But I was able to look past all of that. I knew that I could take anything and make it beautiful. Plus, I had a good feeling being in there and the next day, I took Tre to look at it. Tre walked from the front office to the back office, then through the hallway.

"Is this it?" he asked.

"Yeah!" I said. I think my enthusiasm confused him 'cause he frowned.

"What is this?" he asked.

"This is Miracle Home Care," I told him. "This is gonna be my office."

"You want to open it up over here?" he said as if he couldn't believe it.

"Yeah," I said. "I want to start small. I don't want to jump out there big. I have a vision, but I've got to grow it. Especially since I'm not working with much money."

"Okay," he said, shaking his head. "If this is what you want."

I figured that Tre just didn't get it, but my mom would. So the next day I took her over to the building and she did the same thing that Tre did. She frowned as she walked from the first office to the back office, then through the hallway.

"This is Miracle Home Care," I said.

My mother wasn't as nice as Tre. She said, "Shicka, I just don't see it."

I was shocked because my mother was always so positive about everything when it came to my dream. But, I didn't listen to Tre or my mom. I could see it and that was all that mattered. I had to start somewhere and I knew this space was only going to be temporary.

So, I started my business right in that office. I got in there with a pail of water, and Clorox and Lysol and I cleaned it up real good. Then, I went to Goodwill and got a desk, a chair, and a filing cabinet. I went to the Dollar Store and I picked up a few little decorations.

A week later, I was in business. And right from that office, which was not in the best part of town, I started Miracle Home Care. I went right to work. Every day, I made phone calls, every week, I put ads in the paper. I walked around the neighborhood passing out flyers. I walked the streets, talking to anybody, stopping everybody, telling them all about my business. I walked until my feet hurt. I walked until I had no more flyers.

I know I had to look a sight, being out there like that. I had to look funny to other people, but I didn't care. All kinds of people were looking at me and staring at me. One day when I was passing out flyers, a car honked at me. When I turned, I saw Keisha, a girl I knew from high school.

"What you doing, Shicka?" she yelled out her window, then started laughing as she drove away in her new Honda.

If she was trying to humiliate me, I didn't care because I knew God had His hand on my life. I knew it wasn't going to be easy. But I kept on passing out those flyers, and making those phone calls, and placing those ads. Still, nothing was happening.

"Shicka, maybe we need to move," my mother said one day. "I think that's why you're not getting any clients because of where you're located."

So even though I wasn't sure, I moved to Coral Park Drive, which was a much better location. First of all, we weren't in an alley, across from a strip club. I was on a main road where people could see the sign—Miracle Home Care—much better.

But after a year of being in the new location, I had only added one client. After two years that's all I had—two clients.

Times were so hard. The seven hundred dollars was gone, but I kept at it because I knew down in my soul that this was right. It wouldn't have been so hard if the struggle was just mine. But it wasn't. The struggle belonged to my whole family.

Tre was still in the streets hustling, trying to make something happen for us. And he ended up getting arrested again—this time for violation of his probation.

And my kids had to struggle, too.

Even though I was working the business hard, there were times when the money ran out and we didn't have much of anything. I remember coming home one night, only to find a jug of water, half a loaf of bread and a couple of slices of lunch meat in the refrigerator. That was it.

I cried as I pulled out the meat and bread. This was all that I had to feed my kids. As I made those sandwiches, all I could do was cry and wonder what was going on. All the work I was putting in, everything that I was doing, and this was all that I could give to my children.

I was trying to sniff back my tears when LaMiracle came into the kitchen.

"Mama, are you okay?" my six-year-old daughter asked me.

"Yeah," I said, turning away from her so that she wouldn't see me crying.

She walked over to where I was standing and looked up at me. "We're gonna be all right," she told me.

I tried to smile as I cut the sandwich in half. "Here you go," I said as I gave the sandwich to her.

She sat down at the table, then looked up at me. "Mama, are you gonna eat?"

"No, that's all right, you go ahead, baby."

My little girl shook her head. "Mama, eat a piece of my sandwich 'cause I know you're hungry. I'm not gonna be satisfied until you eat a piece of my sandwich."

I had to fight not to start crying all over again. I just wanted to hug my daughter, but I took a small corner of her sandwich just so that she would eat. "Here you go," I said, handing the sandwich back to her.

"Mama, things are gonna be better. You work so hard for us. Thank you."

This was coming from the mouth of a babe. She was just six. I grabbed my daughter and sat her down on my lap. I didn't even try to hide it anymore. With tears rolling down my face, I said, "Miracle, right now it's hard, it's tough. But, I promise you with everything in my body, we're going to live good one day. You and your brother are never gonna want for nothing. I'm doing this for you. You're young right now and you might not understand it all. But one day, you will. And one day, everything you come and tell me that you want, I'm going to be able to give it to you."

She looked up at me. "I know, Mama." She nodded and then she wrapped her little arms around my neck.

I squeezed her as tight as I could. My daughter filled me with such encouragement that night. It was my kids that gave me my strength and they were my motivation. I didn't want them to go through any of the things that I'd gone through growing up. They truly were at the center of why I was doing all of this.

LaMiracle's words were further affirmation for me that God was in this with me. But that didn't mean life got any easier. In fact, that was just the beginning of just how hard it was going to be.

CHAPTER 31

With Tre away in jail on the probation violation, I knew I couldn't do it anymore. That was when I decided to tell my mother everything. She knew how slow things were with the business, but I hadn't told her how I was struggling at home.

"I don't have any money for anything," I told her. "We don't have any food, the lights are about to be turned off, and I think they're going to repossess my car soon." "Oh, my God!" my mother said. "I didn't know all of that. I thought you had some money saved."

I shook my head. "I didn't want you to know, but I only started the business with seven hundred dollars."

"Oh, Shicka!" my mother said, sounding so sad.

"I really gave it a good try, Mama, but I don't think I can do it anymore. I think I'm gonna close it down and get a job."

"No!" my mother said. "I know this is what you're supposed to be doing. We just have to get someone in there to anoint

Miracle Home Care." My mother said that as if she was sure that was the solution.

I didn't want to shoot down what my mother said. I didn't want to tell her that I had prayed and so I didn't know what more prayers were going to do. I didn't tell her any of that. I was just going to let her do whatever she wanted to do.

While I sat there in her kitchen, she called one of her cousins who was a pastor.

"I need you to come down here and pray over Shicka's business. She's doing God's work and we need to have her business prayed over and anointed."

My mother hung up, and she told me that her cousin was going to meet us down at my office first thing in the morning. That night, I didn't have any expectations, but the next morning, I woke up with a little hope in my heart.

When her cousin walked into my office, he came in the door praying. At first, he just walked around, looking at everything from the desk to the file cabinets. Then, he turned to me and said, "Ain't nobody give you this vision but God."

I was shaking when he said that—that was the truth.

His voice boomed through the office when he said, "I want you to right now to get on your knees 'cause we're about to start shouting and praying up in here. The enemy is trying to come at you any kind of way. He's trying to use your husband, he's trying to use anything that he can.

"But I'm gonna tell you something. After today, the enemy no longer lives in this building. He no longer lives in your home. He's no longer around your kids. You are Abraham's seed and you fixin' to prosper, right now in the name of Jesus!"

My cousin got to praying. He walked around that building and touched everything as he prayed. He prayed over the walls,

214 | Shashicka Tyre-Hill

the filing cabinets, and the phones. He touched the windows and the doors. He anointed that entire place with oil.

While my cousin was praying, my mother and I were shouting. We had church up in there. For about an hour we just walked through that office, following her cousin, praying and praising.

Well, we had sent the praises up. And the blessings came pouring down. I'd only had two clients when my mother's cousin walked into my office, but in that next week, I had ten clients. A month after that, I had fifteen clients.

The money was pouring in. My business was booming. I had more clients, I hired home care workers, I was able to take care of home. There was so much money coming in. I had more money in my bank account than I had ever had in my life.

Life was good.

Then, it all stopped. It kind of blew up in my face. Because with all of that money coming in, I just didn't know what to do. So, I did the only thing I knew—I spent it all.

And I sent my thriving business into a downward fall.

CHAPTER 32

The clients were coming in, the money was pouring in and business was just booming! I was so excited. All I wanted to do was to see Miracle Home Care continue to grow. So I kept my eyes on anything that would help me make my home care business even more successful.

The first thing I did was hire an administrator—someone who could help me with all the paperwork, with scheduling, with marketing, with everything because the clients were coming in so quickly.

Then, I looked for ways to really expand my business. I wanted to get our name out there. I didn't have to look far. All kinds of salespeople contacted me. They told me all kinds of things—how their services could help me become the number one company in Georgia.

That sounded wonderful to me. I was trying to be on the fast track, so I did all kinds of advertising: newspaper and radio ads. And then there was the Yellow Pages. I wanted to make sure that whenever anyone was looking up home care, they saw Miracle Home Care.

It was all so expensive, especially the Yellow Pages. But, it was going to be worth it because my business would keep growing.

Months went by, and clients were continuing to come in. But then, I began to notice...something was happening to the money. As more clients came in, I had to hire more employees. And I began to see the money was dwindling, dwindling, and dwindling until I was down to just about nothing.

There was a major thing that I didn't take into account. While the clients were coming in fast, the money wasn't coming in as fast. There were many clients who didn't want to pay upfront. They wanted to pay after services were already rendered.

I had several twenty-four hour clients who paid only once a month, but in the meantime, I needed three aides to provide the care for them around the clock. That was happening over and over again. And so, I was taking the money from the bank to pay the employees, and to pay the bills...and to advertise to expand the business. And soon, I was down to nothing. Seriously. Nothing.

I had all of these clients and not enough money to keep the business going.

I knew I had to do something—and quick. So, I went to Brunswick and took business management classes. In the classes, I learned everything from not only how to budget my money, to what kind of advertising my business really needed.

One of the biggest lessons I learned in that class though was how to pay myself.

"So many businesses fail because the owners are overpaying themselves," the instructor said. "When you have a certain amount of money coming in, you should only pay yourself a percentage of that."

She taught us not to take too much out of the business.

"Allow your business to grow. Pay yourself, but make sure that you've set it up so that your business will continue to expand."

So, that was one of the first changes I made. Instead of paying myself $600 a week, which is what I'd been doing, I dropped it to $400 a week and kept it there for two years—even after I was back on my feet financially. I cancelled all of that unnecessary advertising that was eating away at my money and I learned to really manage the business and the money since I had the kind of business where sometimes we had to do the work before we were paid.

Learning how to really manage money didn't just help me with Miracle Home Care. I learned how to manage money at home, too. As the business was growing, there were times when I had to go without new clothes and new shoes. I had to forego getting my nails done and my hair done. I had to do all of that so that I could build up my company.

Getting control of my finances really helped me to turn it around. I was able to triple the money I had in the bank, making sure that I could survive even by having to pay my employees before I was paid by the clients.

The business was continuing to expand and by the time a year had passed from when I took the business classes, Miracle Home Care had doubled in sales to almost $100,000.

All I needed was a little education and I was able to turn that business around.

CHAPTER 33

Miracle Home Care was doing well and I began to think about other business opportunities. I wasn't actively out looking for anything, but one night when I was driving home, I saw a woman walking on the edge of the road. It was pouring rain and the woman looked to be in her forties, so, I pulled over.

I rolled down my window. "Do you need a ride?"

"Oh, thank you," she said and jumped into my car. She was still saying, "Thank you, thank you," over and over again.

"Where are you going?" I asked.

She gave me her address and I looked at her out of the corner of my eye. "Where are you from?"

"Jamaica."

"Oh, my goodness. I love Jamaican food." I told her about one of my favorite restaurants that was down in Savannah. "I would love to open a Jamaican restaurant."

"Really?" she said. "I want to open a restaurant, too."

I'm telling you, I didn't know this woman from anyone. She was a complete stranger. But she wasn't a stranger by the time I dropped her off at home. We arranged to meet the next day to really discuss the idea of a restaurant.

When, I dropped her off, I was about to drive off when I yelled out the window, "Hey, what's your name?"

"Hope."

"I'm Shashicka," I said.

She grinned. "Nice to meet you."

We had done all of that talking and hadn't even asked each other's names. But, there was something about Hope that I trusted and when we met the next day at my office, I knew I was right.

Just like everything else in my life, I made the decision to move forward and Hope and I put all the plans together. We found a small space on 4th Street, one of the main streets where there would be a lot of traffic.

This was going to be new in Brunswick, but like Miracle Home Care, I didn't want to go big. I wanted it to be mostly a take-out place. So the space we rented only had room for two tables. Most of the space was the kitchen.

Opening Caribbean Express wasn't a huge investment for me. By the time we opened, I'd invested about four thousand dollars into it. And it was a great investment. Caribbean Express was so different, that for the first few weeks, we had nothing but long, long lines. Even after the newness wore off, the business continued to do well.

But it was tough for me because it was so different from Miracle Home Care. I ran my health care business almost on a shoe-string budget. The restaurant was the complete opposite. It had high overhead. Besides the salaries that I had to pay (I was used to that part), the supplies for the business were expensive. We had to have the food and the seasonings and the plates and carryout cartons. There were so many things that I hadn't known about or thought about. It didn't take me long, only about nine months, to realize that this wasn't my type of business. I didn't even have the restaurant for a year before I decided that I didn't want it as an investment.

But it was still doing well and Hope really wanted to keep it. So, I sold it to her. Not for very much money—though I did make back double my initial investment, plus the profits from the months that I had the business.

Selling the restaurant gave me a chance to invest a bit in my family. The home that we had been living in was nice enough—if you didn't mind the roaches and the rats. We had a major problem with rats primarily because our house was back in the woods. So even though it was a nice floor plan with four bedrooms, it was a mess.

Once I sold the restaurant, Tre and I decided to move into another home on the North End of town. We bought a beautiful two-story, five-bedroom, three-and-a-half bath home with a large backyard and in a much better neighborhood. We didn't sell the house we'd moved from at first—we rented it out for about a year. But when I did sell the home, we were able to make a nice profit on it. Nice enough to buy another rental property and put money in the bank. I earned so much from renting that within a year, I'd bought three more rental properties.

I turned my focus back to Miracle Home Care and became part of the Community Care Program. I found out about Community Care through one of my former clients who had just been approved for Community Care, and finding this program was a blessing. Community Care is a program where the government pays. The clients came to me from the State.

When I filled out the application and was accepted into that program, things just started happening for me in a big way. I'd already had a large clientele, but it grew even more. The State was sending me so many clients it was a challenge to keep up.

From the outside, everything looked wonderful, but it wasn't all good. I had to deal with a lot of insurance companies and took quite a few losses. Like with one insurance company (that I won't name) that was supposed to pay me $90 for every time a health care worker went to assist their client. Well, they only paid me $20. I'd already paid my aides $65, so not only did I not earn anything, I lost money.

Most of the insurance companies paid, but the challenge was, they paid three or four months later. So, I had to really learn how to manage the business and manage the finances. But at the end of the year, Miracle Home Care had grown another 35 percent. Sales ended at almost $130,000. And in Brunswick, Georgia, that was considered a very, very successful business.

But God had even greater, even bigger plans for me and Miracle Home Care. There was no way for me to just sit back and enjoy the fruits of my labor because I hadn't seen anything yet!

CHAPTER 34

Everything in my life was going so well. Not only was Miracle Home Care doing well, but the rental properties were bringing in income, too. I was able to provide for my children in a way that I hadn't been able to before...and it seemed like everything was going to go well forever.

Then, there was Tre.

Not only was my business doing well, but things were better with Tre, too. He was much more supportive to me, and he seemed to be home more. But apparently, that didn't change his ways. He was still running around with different women.

I received another one of those phone calls. From a woman. Who told me that she was pregnant from Tre.

Oh, my God! Not again. That was all that I could think.

It was so devastating to hear those words...again.

Of course, the first thing I did was ask Tre. Of course, the first thing he did was to deny it.

We argued about it back and forth, but there was nothing I could do when he told me that it was all a lie. So, I had to go on and pretend that I'd never received the call. I pretended that everything was fine with my husband.

But the truth was, things were never the same after that. It had been a long time since I'd trusted Tre fully and now even the little bit of trust I had was gone.

It was a weird place to be. I loved Tre and we were in a better place because he was supporting me with my business and helping me with the children and overall being a great husband. But I didn't trust him. I couldn't.

And then, he did something so wonderful.

"I want to adopt Miracle," he said. "She's really my daughter. She has been since she was little."

This was something Tre and I had talked about because all LaMiracle knew was Tre. But when she turned nine or ten, she began to have questions.

"Mama, Xavier's last name is Hill, and Dad's last name is Hill and sometimes, your last name is Hill. Why is my last name Tyre?"

"Miracle, my last name is Tyre, too."

I had done that on purpose. I used Tyre sometimes, even after Tre and I were married because I didn't want LaMiracle to ever feel different or left out. So, I kept Tyre because of her.

"You and I are Tyres and Xavier and Tre are Hills."

That answer would satisfy LaMiracle, but only for a little while. She was a smart child, and the difference was really beginning to bother her.

We'd have these discussions often, and finally she told me, "Mama, I don't want to be a Tyre anymore. I want to be a Hill."

Over the years, I'd told Tre about my conversations with LaMiracle and he had always done whatever he could to make sure that LaMiracle knew she was loved and a part of our family.

So, when Tre said that he wanted to adopt LaMiracle, I knew he really meant it. He had been taking care of her, supporting her and loving her as if she was his own. But I also knew that timing is everything. With the call I'd received from this woman, Tre was thinking this was a good time to bring this up, especially with the way he knew I felt. He knew I didn't trust him anymore. And he could probably feel that my love for him had changed. I'd gone from being in love with him to just loving him. And for me, that was a big difference.

"I really want to do this, Shicka."

I nodded. "You are her daddy."

"Well then, let's go ahead and get it done."

I started the process to get the paperwork going, and even though I was happy that Tre loved LaMiracle enough to do this, that didn't change how I was feeling about Tre and all these women. But there was nothing I could do about the women, so this time, I wasn't even going to entertain the situation. After Tre denied and denied it, I decided that whether it was true or not, I wasn't going to let it mess with me. I had a growing business and I had to stay focused on that and my children.

Clients were coming in fast from the State. Besides the clients in Brunswick, the State started sending me clients from St. Mary's County in Kingsland. There were quite a few, and it became a challenge to find staff for that area since Brunswick was an hour away from Kingsland. So, I spoke with the case manager with Community Care and she suggested that I open up an office in Kingsland.

At first, I didn't want to do it. After having taken those business management courses, I was always so careful with my money, so careful with my planning, so careful with my expanding. But the more I thought about it, the more that I knew the case worker was right. An office in Kingsland would allow me to get the employees that I needed to handle all the cases. And if I had an office there, I would probably get more cases.

I really made my decision when we found out that Tre had to go to the PDC—Probation Detention Center. He was going to have to do ten to twelve months for once again violating probation. He hadn't been showing up to his probation officer, he hadn't been doing his community service. So now, he was going to have to do his time.

This time, I wasn't even worried about Tre being away. It gave me time to focus on my business and not have to worry about all the other stuff. I put all of my energy into Kingsland. But just like I'd done with my first location, I opened up with a very small office. It was so small, there was just enough room for two desks. I had an administrator who was going to run the office since I couldn't be there every single day and an administrative assistant.

I was blessed in so many ways with this new office, especially with my administrator. Donna was an acquaintance of my administrator in Brunswick and she had home care experience and just happened to be available.

Opening up the second location helped me to begin to take my business to a whole 'nother level. We doubled and ended that year with almost a quarter of a million dollars in sales—all because of a second location.

Now I knew, there were big things in the future for Miracle Home Care.

CHAPTER 35

While Tre was at the PDC, I visited him just about every weekend. It was an hour drive and every Saturday I would make that trip. I only took the kids with me two or three times. They were missing their father, so I had to take them a couple of times. But I never wanted my kids to spend too much time in a place like that.

Tre finally came home in February of 2009 and he came home to something beautiful. The adoption of Miracle was final. Tre had signed the papers while he was away and LaMiracle had approved it, too.

I had talked to my daughter about it while Tre was in PDC. Even though she had been talking about her last name and even though she thought of Tre as her father, I knew adoption was a big step. So, I wanted her to really think about it and be part of the decision.

"Now, Miracle, this is not something that you have to do. I want you to feel okay with it. You will always be a part of us and a part of this family no matter what name you have. I don't want you to do it because you think this is what I want you to do."

But, she was so excited. "No, Mama, that's my daddy. I really want to do this."

So when Tre came home, it was official. We still had to go to the county to have LaMiracle's name officially changed to Hill.

When Miracle told me, "I feel so complete now because we're all Hills," that's when I officially changed my name, too. Because like I said, I'd always kept Tyre for Miracle's sake. But, I didn't have to do that anymore.

So the two of us went to have our names changed together and it was quite a celebration at home.

After being away for ten months, Tre was once again very loving and very supportive. It was easy to look at him and really see him as my husband with the way he was acting toward me. And that made it easier for me to look at and handle the situation of Tre with this other woman and this supposed baby.

I talked to Tre about the situation because even though I had tried to pretend, it just wasn't going to go away. The woman kept calling and when Tre came home, I wanted it handled.

"Are you this baby's father?" I asked him.

He shook his head. "I'm gonna tell you the truth. I don't think so, but I don't know. What I do know is that you're my wife and I love you. The only person I want to be with is you."

It was hard, but I decided that if Tre did have another child on the outside, then that child was going to be a part of us, a part of our family.

So after talking it over with Tre, I convinced him that we all needed to meet. It took a bit of encouraging, but finally we had the girl come over—with her baby.

It was a cordial meeting. I did most of the talking and I did most of the talking to her since I'd already talked to Tre. I told her, "Listen, this is the situation. If this is his child, then I need to be involved and know what's going on." I made it clear how I wanted everything handled. "You don't have to call Tre. I need to be the one that you call and we will make sure together that you have what you need. There doesn't need to be any contact between the two of you because I already don't trust you or the situation. Do you understand?"

"Yes," she told me.

I looked over at Tre. "Yeah," he said.

When she left, I was sure that everybody had the same understanding. But of course, one day, I found out that they were contacting each other without me knowing anything about it. So, I shut it down. I told Tre that I didn't want to have anything to do with the situation anymore. And I went back to what I knew best...I went back to my business. I went back to focusing on my business and my children.

My mind was on my business when I met a young woman who was dating my cousin. Sabrina was really cool, and she and I developed a friendship. She would come over and we would hang out and because of her, I met Sabrina's sister, Charlene. Charlene was in school to become a nurse and just like her sister, Charlene and I became friends.

One day, the three of us, along with my mother, took a road trip to Jacksonville. This wasn't just any ol' road trip...my mother had finally decided to get married again. She and Brian had been together for three years and when she told me that, I was thrilled. For this wedding, I wanted to do everything that I could to help, so I called up Sabrina and Charlene, and then the three of us rode with my mom to Jacksonville to find her the best wedding dress ever.

In the car ride down, all my mother could do was talk about Miracle Home Care. You would think she would have been focused on her wedding, but she wasn't. She was just so proud of me and she always let everyone know.

"I really think you need to do a location in Jessup," she said. "I think that would be a great place for an office."

I didn't say anything out loud, but I didn't agree with my mother. First of all, I didn't think there were many old people out there and I wasn't interested in another location—that would be three. Two were enough for me.

"Wow! You're really doing great things, Shicka," Charlene said. "I think an office in Jessup would be great and if you need me to help, I can help you. That's something that I always wanted to do."

"Okay," I said. "We'll talk."

I don't know how serious I was about it, but over the next few days, Charlene called me just about every day. Finally, I began to think about it, too. I told her that she'd have to go through some training.

"No problem," she said.

The next week, Charlene was in Brunswick!

There was nothing I could do except open up in Jessup—all because of Charlene. She encouraged me to do it.

So, within a month, we had the office open. Like I'd done before, I opened it small. There was only Charlene and an administrative assistant, Sonya, there.

But Jessup didn't take off like we did in Kingsland. For three months, there was nothing. No clients at all.

At the beginning of the fourth month, Charlene called me. "Shicka, I'm so sorry, but I can't do this anymore," she said. "You're going to have to find someone else."

"Okay," I said. "Let me come down there and we'll figure this out."

On the ride to Jessup, I felt really bad. I had already felt like Jessup was not a good area and now I'd brought Charlene into it. But, I had to convince her that these things take time. Now that I was in Jessup, I wasn't ready to give up. Imagine if I had given up in the first year with Miracle Home Care?

When I got to Jessup, I talked to Charlene, but it was Sonya who made the most difference.

"I know this is going to work," Sonya said. "I just know it. I know that we're going to do it."

I nodded like I agreed, though the thought was still in the back of my mind that Jessup wasn't a good area.

Sonya said, "What we need to do is pray!"

Well, that had worked for me before, so with Sonya's lead, we stood in that office, and the three of us held hands and prayed. When, I left that office I think all three of us had just a little more hope.

The next week, a woman from Source walked into the Jessup office. Source is the same thing as Community Care Program. They provide clients from the State as well. It's just a different program run by a different division of the government.

The lady from Source looked around, spoke to Charlene and Sonya and told them that Source wanted to send us clients. The moment the lady left the office, Charlene called me so excited.

"You need to come down here and talk to these people," she told me.

"I'll be there tomorrow!"

I went straight to the Source office and met with the case manager.

"We have about eighteen clients that we want to send to you," she told me. "These clients want to leave this other agency that's not doing well with them and we don't have anywhere to send them."

"I'll take them."

She laughed. "All right. You need to get on this program."

The next day, we began intaking the clients. Like the case manager said, they sent us eighteen people. I was so happy, Charlene was so happy, Sonya was so happy. We got to work hiring people and we serviced those clients for the first month.

At the end of the month, when it was time to bill Source, I called the case manager.

"How do I bill for these?" I asked her.

She was quiet for a moment. "Oh, my God. You have to put in an application. You have to go through the State." She listed a whole bunch of other stuff, but mentally, I had already checked out. You mean to tell me we had done all of this and we weren't going to get paid?

"And then, the State has to approve you," the case manager went on. "It can sometimes take two years for that to happen."

"Oh, my God. I've been servicing these people for the past month," I said, very upset. "I've put out all of this money, we've had fourteen aides covering them, and now you're telling me I have to go through all of this?"

"I'm so sorry," the case manager said. "I can give you the number to call."

I wanted to scream, but I knew that wasn't going to do any good. I had to take care of business.

So, I called the number she gave me, got someone on the phone and said, "This is Shashicka Hill. I'm with Miracle Home Care," and then, I went on to explain the situation. "I'm not going to be able to continue to do these clients for free," I said when I finished explaining everything to her.

"Oh, no, you're not going to have to do anything for free. You said that you're servicing these clients right now, right?"

"Yes, ma'am."

"Okay, then. I'm going to go ahead and process everything now and in thirty days you'll receive payment and then you'll be able to go back and bill for what you've already done."

I wanted to jump up and do another praise dance. *Thank you, God!* was all I kept saying to myself.

What normally took two years, I ended up doing in a month. Because I was already servicing these clients, I was on the Source Program thirty days after I spoke to the State.

Once we had all of those eighteen clients settled and paid for, I went back to Jessup, put on my tennis shoes and some jeans and we hit the streets for more clients. I wanted people to know that they could be eligible for the Source program, which serviced people who made less than $600 a month. So, we went to churches, to the Salvation Army, to Manna Houses, we passed out flyers—we did a little bit of everything. It was all Street Marketing to me. We went into the rural areas and started talking to people. People referred us to folks they knew who were sick and/or shut-in. We knocked on doors, gave them the information. We let everyone know that Miracle Home Care was there! And very likely, they could get on the Source program.

That Street Marketing more than doubled the number of clients and doubled the business in Jessup.

The great thing about the Source program was that it wasn't just in Jessup. Source covered a number of counties. So once we handled Jessup, we hit the streets in other counties, giving people the same information.

The Source and the Street Marketing helped Miracle Home Care have a really good year. We ended the year with three offices and more than $400,000 in sales.

And because of the Source program and all the marketing we'd done, I decided to think about opening another location—this time in Savannah. We had already started getting clients in that area and just like with what happened in Kingsland, it was hard to staff since Savannah was a little ways away. So, I was ready to go to Savannah.

But that dream had to be put on hold for a moment because I got another call...this time, from my godbrother.

CHAPTER 36

"Shicka," my godbrother, Teddy, said sounding kind of frantic on the phone, "they're getting ready to take my barbershop and my license away from me."

"What's going on?"

Teddy told me how he was behind on all the bills and how he had major fines from the State. He explained how he'd been trying to help out other guys who didn't have licenses and whenever the State came in for inspection and caught them there, he'd get fined. "So with the fines and all the other bills, I just can't do it anymore. I really need your help."

"Okay," I said. "Come into the office so that we can talk."

The next day, Teddy was there first thing and when he sat down in my office, he told me what he wanted me to do. "Just come in and take it over, Shicka. That's all I want."

I shook my head. "That's not something I do. I don't cut hair. That's not my dream. Plus, right now, I'm in the process of opening an office in Savannah. I'm sorry, but I can't help you."

Teddy put his head down. "Shicka," he began in a low voice, "I wouldn't even come to you if I didn't really need your help. You've got to help me."

I felt my heart softening again. I felt that thing that God had given to me. That need and desire to help people when I could, especially my family.

It only took me a couple of seconds to say, "I tell you what. I'll put Savannah on hold so that we can do this."

For the first time since my godbrother had walked in, he smiled.

I was going to make sure that his barbershop was successful, and that meant that I was going to apply the same principles that made me successful with Miracle Home Care.

I dropped everything that I was doing with Miracle Home Care and Teddy and I went around town and started looking for a building for his barbershop. We found a space but when we went inside, that place needed so much work it was ridiculous.

"I don't know, Teddy. This looks like it's gonna cost a lot of money to go in and do this."

"I think we can do it," Teddy said. "This is a good location, we'll get traffic. I'm telling you, this is the place."

"I tell you what. Let's get a meeting with the barbers that you have now. I want to see how committed they are before I put any money into this."

What I was trying to figure out was whether or not this business was going to be profitable. I was only interested in something that was going to make me money.

Teddy didn't waste any time. He called me that night and had set up the meeting for the next day. We met at my office in Coral Park with all five guys: Teddy, Brian, Travis, Buster, and Sam.

I got right to the point. "I want to help my godbrother, but this is something that I'm going to have to put a lot of money into in order to make it work. And the booth rents that you're paying now, won't help to cover it." I paused, waiting for one of them to say something, but no one said anything. So, I said, "I'm going to have to raise the booth rents, but I promise you that I will put everything into this to make it successful for you and me."

They looked at each other and nodded.

"We really want this to work," Travis said.

The rest of the guys nodded with Travis.

"Okay, then," I said. "I'm gonna go ahead and invest my money."

The guys were excited and started telling me everything that they wanted. They wanted real barber chairs and TVs wrapped around the wall. I took notes and agreed to everything. I knew that if I wanted this business to work, the guys would have to be proud of their space. And, I knew that if I gave them everything, they would work hard.

After the guys left, I told Teddy, "Now, the only reason I'm doing this is for you, so one day, you're going to buy this back from me."

"That's a deal," he said.

Then, I went in and got on it. I put in the orders for the equipment that was needed, I ordered all the electronics while the contractors went in and did their work—from painting the walls to fixing the floors.

Within a month, we opened up the doors to Celebrity Status. From the moment we opened our doors, Celebrity Status became the hottest barbershop in Brunswick, Georgia. It is young and hip and with the seven barbers (we added one more), it's still going strong.

CHAPTER 37

Six months after I opened up Celebrity Status and got that business going, I was able to move ahead with opening up the office for Miracle Home Care in Savannah. I was anxious to get this office opened since, like I said, we already had clients there. I needed to at least maintain that business and then grow it the way I had grown all the other offices.

Just like with all of my other offices, I was able to get an administrator in Savannah through someone I already knew. My assistant's cousin, Nicole, lived in Savannah and after I met her and we developed a good business relationship, Nicole came down to Brunswick for training.

Now with four offices: Coral Park, Kingsland, Jessup and Savannah, plus Celebrity Status, I decided that I was going to focus on making sure these four offices were strong.

Of course, I couldn't sit still for long. My offices were not only doing well, they were growing and I was ready to step forward so that Miracle Home Care could grow even more.

Atlanta was the city that I kept hearing about. People kept prophesizing over me, telling me that I was going to have an office in Atlanta. But just the mention of that city put fear in me. Maybe it was because of all I went through when I was first going to get my license to start Miracle Home Care. Whatever it was, I didn't think an office in Atlanta would fit with what I was doing. It was four hours away from Brunswick, which was too far to me. Everything else, at this point, was only an hour, maybe an hour and a half from me. That was important in case anything happened, I could get there quickly.

But even with that, I couldn't get Atlanta out of my mind and I started thinking about what God had done for me to this point. Everything had been about faith and stepping out and maybe Atlanta was a test of my faith, too. Maybe I needed to step out on faith and do this thing.

Now mind you, I didn't have any clients in Atlanta. There really wasn't any reason for me to be there—except, I really wanted to have Miracle Home Care grow and Atlanta would be the first major city. I had visions of my company being all over the country and going to Atlanta would be the first step for me to see if I could make it happen.

So, Atlanta it was. That was going to be where I would have my next office.

I put together a plan—I was going to have to be there at least for a few months, maybe even a year. Then once I had my plan, I put together a team to go with me to Atlanta: my mom, and three of my friends: Beatty, Estella, and Sherri. Of course, I took Miracle and Xavier with me, too, since it was summer. And Tre came down whenever he could.

We were going to be down there for a while so I rented a house for all of us. And then, we hit the streets, doing that Street

Marketing that always worked for me. We marketed for about three months and at first, there was nothing. We'd been there for all of that time, and we didn't have any clients.

Unfortunately, I let fear take over and once again, I was scared. *Was this going to be the first location where I failed?* All kinds of negative thoughts filled my head: *I knew I shouldn't have come to Atlanta. Why did I think I could make it happen in Atlanta?*

As the days rolled on, it became harder and harder not to be discouraged. One night, I was sitting on the stairs in the house after I thought everyone had gone to bed. I just wanted some time to be alone—to have my own pity party. I was sitting there crying when I heard footsteps behind me.

I turned around and when I saw Miracle, I tried to wipe my tears away so that she wouldn't see them.

But like always, I couldn't fool my child. I guess she had seen me cry too many times before. "What's wrong, Mama?" she asked as she sat on the step next to me.

I took a moment before I told her, "I think I'm gonna give up. I've got to give up."

She shook her head. "No, Mama. You ain't never gave up on nothing before. Don't give up. It's gonna happen. It always happens."

"You just don't understand," I said. I was thinking that Miracle was just a child. How could she know all that I was going through? How could she know the pain of feeling so defeated?

"Mama...it's a miracle. You can do it. It's a miracle and it's gonna happen. Just have faith. You know what it takes."

I looked up at my child and when I did, it was like a light shined on her face. That's when I got it.

The Source!

I was already on that program. What was I doing? I was trying to market and reach people when I already had what I needed. I was trying to reinvent something that I already had!

Sitting on the steps, I could hear God as clear as day saying, *Shicka, I already gave you the gift. When that lady knocked on the door and told you that she had eighteen clients for you that was a gift. So why are you trying to go out when the gift is right here in your hands?*

I stood up and hugged my baby so tight. Once again, my baby had told me something that I should've already known. I couldn't wait for morning to come. The next day, I was at the Source before the doors even opened.

After I talked to the lady for a little while, she said, "Yeah, we got plenty of clients for you! Are you in Atlanta now?"

From that day, we had clients! I had to find a location right away, which I did since I already had my eye on something. Sherri became the administrator and we got to work!

For the next few weeks, I spent the time training Sherri and hiring aides to start taking care of the clients that were coming from the Source. The office was thriving, we were so busy and we had another success on our hands.

We had only been open a few weeks, when I received a call from my administrator, Jocelyn, in Brunswick.

"Shicka, you need to come back," she said, sounding very excited—but not in a good way.

"Why? What's going on?"

"The State is here and they're getting ready to go through all your paperwork to make sure that everything is in compliance."

I rushed out of the office leaving everyone there and hopped a plane as quickly as I could to get back Brunswick. Compliance?

What did they mean? I had never had an official visit like this before.

But the visit turned out very well. The state found that I was in compliance, and after that visit, I decided to even take the Source courses so that I could learn everything that I needed to know to take my business to the top.

It worked because by the end of the year, I reached another milestone. With the help of the Atlanta office, Miracle Home Care closed the year as a million dollar business.

That should have been very exciting to me and it was, but I still had issues at home. It was Tre again. It was a girl again. It was another claim that Tre was the father of her baby.

But this time, I wasn't going to entertain it at all. I pushed it out of my mind and heart—it was just not relevant to me. What was going on on the outside just didn't affect my household.

While I say that it didn't affect my household, it did affect my heart. Trust issues? We had them big time. There was absolutely no trust. And without trust, every day we grew further apart. It was all on me, not on Tre at all. He was trying his best to be supportive, helping me with my business. But as each day passed, I started feeling that I just couldn't do it. I just couldn't be with him anymore. I had finally, finally, finally reached the end of my rope. I was just fed up. I'd done all I could to stay. I'd done all I could to please God knowing that He hates divorce, but I was at the point where it was over for me.

I spoke to an attorney and filed for divorce.

Then, I told Tre that I was done. I was really done.

But Tre was the one who wouldn't give up on us.

"Shicka, I know I've done a lot of things wrong. We can work this out."

I shook my head. "I can't because I've lost all trust. How can we stay married with no trust?"

"But, I love you and I'm not going anywhere. I've changed. I really have and I'm just asking you to give me this chance, give us this chance because I'm not leaving. I'm not going. I'm not giving up."

"It's too late. I've already filed."

"I don't care what you say," Tre said. "I'm not giving up."

I didn't want to hear what he had to say, but what was interesting was the timing of all of this. Tre's cousin, who's a very spiritual man surprised us with a visit. When he came to our house, Tre told him what was going on and his cousin sat us down and talked to us together.

"I have watched y'all for many years and even with everything, I can tell you that y'all are meant to be. And you need to understand this...the enemy comes in and tries to destroy what God has put together." Then, he turned to Tre. "You have a strong wife who loves you. She's always supported you. You cannot allow the outside to come in and break up what you have."

Tre said, "I don't want to do that."

His cousin asked me, "Do you love him? Do you love your husband?"

"Yeah, I love him, but to be honest, I'm not in love with him."

"Well, that's understandable, but this relationship can be fixed. What y'all need to do is get in a church home and y'all need to start praying and working this thing out together."

I have to admit, I was skeptical. I mean, really, did he think that was going to change Tre? Did he think that was going to fix our marriage?

Well, Tre's cousin has often been called a prophet and I wasn't ever sure what people meant by that. But it turned out that Tre's cousin was right. Because ever since his cousin spoke to us and we joined Mount Sinai Church, Tre completely changed.

From that talk forward, it was like Tre became a new man. He became the husband that I always desired, the husband that I always dreamed of.

This is going to sound strange, but I think it took all that we went through with all of those other women for us to get to this place where we are now. When I married Tre, he didn't understand what a husband was. His father died when he was seven years old. So, he didn't have that male in his life to direct him and teach him the role of a husband. His grandparents were strong, but they were a lot older and I don't think Tre could relate to his grandfather in that way.

Really, I didn't understand either. I didn't understand the role of a wife. When we talked, really talked, Tre told me that there were times when I made him feel less than a man. He told me that there were times when I made him feel like I didn't even notice him, like I didn't even need him.

I explained to him that I only took control of our life because he was in the streets. I told him that he wasn't really there the way I thought that he should have been. I tried to make it clear that the only way I knew how to handle the situation was to just stay focused on everything that I wanted to do.

But the good thing was that we talked, I mean really talked. And I was able to get my points across to Tre and he explained to me some of the things I should've done. From there, we started understanding each other better. From there, we worked even more closely together. Tre really became a part of my business and I did my best to include him in everything.

And I can honestly say that from there, God truly gave me the best husband in the world. I love him, he loves me and we love each other.

And that is all that anyone else needs to know.

CHAPTER 38

W e were a million-dollar business now, and we were busting at the seams at our Coral Park location. I finally decided to move to a bigger office—I guessed it was time.

Once we were situated in the new "headquarters," I began to think of other ways we could make Miracle Home Care grow. I was looking for businesses that would work well with what I already had.

The first thing that came to my mind was a daycare for adults. I had been getting calls for a while from clients who didn't have insurance and who couldn't afford home health care out of their pockets. But they still had need for my services, just on a daily basis.

So, I started thinking about how I could service those people. I thought about a daycare center where we would have activities and the clients would be fed and taken care of during the day. This would be especially good for people who had elderly parents or other relatives with them. This way, the son or daughter could go to work and not have to worry about their parent.

I got started on opening up that business, but one of the first things I realized was that if I was going to do this, I needed transportation to pick up the adults and bring them to the center. So I bought a bus—Miracle Transportation—that I was just going to use to transport clients to and from the daycare business.

But as soon as I got that bus with the logo and telephone number on it, people started calling and asking if I could take their mother to the doctor or their father to the store. I got so many calls that I had to postpone opening the daycare center and had to focus on the transportation service that helped the elderly and disabled people get around Brunswick.

Like everything else, that transportation business took off, but I still wanted to do the daycare center. I found a building that was just perfect for what I needed. On one side, I could do the adult day care and then on the other side I could do something else that I had dreamed about—assisted living for the elderly.

For me, finding that building was a sign that I just needed to go ahead and do the assisted living, too. So, I did both.

And it was clear that God's hands were on my business and remained there. Because from 2011 to 2012, in that one year, my business tripled. We finished the year with over three million dollars in sales.

It's kind of scary to think of where we can go now. The projections are that we will triple in sales again this year. But whatever we do, I'm ready for it all. Because I know everything that I have has been a gift from God. He's filled my hands with gifts and my life with His miracles. So knowing all of that simply means that I just have to open my arms and accept it all.

And all I want to do now, is give back the way that God has given to me. My desire is to make as much of a difference in people's lives as I can.

So, that's my hope, my desire, and my plan. To continue this journey, this wonderful life that has been filled to the top with miracles and to share it with as many people as I possibly can.

CHAPTER 39

So, that is my story—the good and the bad of it. And, I have to say there has been much more good than bad. Of course, you would read this and say, 'Yes, definitely, there has been more good.' But, I'm not saying that because of the money that I've been blessed with. I'm saying that there's been more good than bad because of God.

God has turned every situation that the devil meant for bad into good. It's beyond the money that I've earned. It's all of the blessings that God has given to me that money could never buy.

First, He blessed me with my beautiful daughter, LaMiracle who was the first miracle in my life. She's been with me longer than anyone, she's seen the good times and the bad. And the bad times didn't matter to her. I cannot count the number of times she comforted me, I can't count the times that she made a difference. And it's because of that unconditional love that she's always given to me, that now, I give her all that I can. Of course,

I love her, but I spoil her a little bit, too. It's okay. She's a good girl. She's a miracle and she's a blessing.

The second blessing that God gave me was Tre. You already know that Tre and I had plenty of bad times and I know that there are many women (and maybe men) who look at all that we've been through and wonder why I'm still with Tre. But you want to know why? Because I know in my heart that he is the husband that God wanted me to have. God never promised easy, He just promised completion. And Tre and I are now complete. I believe that's because Tre and I honored God. We stayed together no matter what, and now I know for sure that what God has put together no man, no woman, no baby, no lies, no fear, no tears...nothing can tear your marriage apart if you rely on The Lord. Sometimes you have to go through the trials to get to the triumphs and that's what's happened with me and Tre.

And not only is Tre a wonderful husband, but he's an amazing father to our children. He loves LaMiracle...oh, my God, he is so good to my daughter, who is his daughter now. He's always treated her like his own and for that I am so grateful. And Tre's a great father to our son, Xavier.

I have a marriage now where my husband loves me with all of his heart, and supports me with all that is in him. I have the husband that little girls hope they will grow up to marry.

And my third blessing is my thirteen-year-old son, Xavier. I am so blessed to be this little man's mother. No matter how well I'm doing financially, he's not the type of child to say, "Mama, I want this," or "Mama, I want that."

Xavier is more likely to say, "Mama, if you have it, that's fine. You don't have to. I understand." He is just the sweetest young man and I'm looking forward to all that God has planned for his life.

My blessings continue because I'm surrounded by the love and support of my family. First, my mother—there is so much to say about her. From the time when we were little and she would do whatever she had to do to take care of us, to her being the reason why I really pursued my dream. Everyone should be blessed to have a mother like mine—one who supports you no matter what.

And there are others—family and friends, who knew me before Miracle Home Care and who loved me even then.

My life has been filled with blessings, with gifts, with miracles. And my hope and prayer is that after reading this book, your life will be filled with nothing but miracles, too!

Miracle Publishing
650 Scranton Road Suite J
Brunswick, GA. 31520

Order Form

Blessings and Miracles $15.00
Shipping/handling (via U.S. Priority Mail) $ 5.00
(NOTE: 2 books in same package 1x SH fee)
Total $20.00

Purchaser Information
Name: _____
Reg #: _____
Address: _____
_____
City: _____ State: _____ Zip: _____

Total Number of Books Ordered: _____

Ship to: (if address is different then purchaser information)
Name: _____
Reg #: _____
Address: _____
_____
City: _____ State: _____ Zip: _____

For orders shipped directly to prisons Publisher deducts 25% off the sale price of the book. Costs are as follows:
Title of Book $11.25
Shipping/handling $ 5.00
Total $16.25

20158508R00136

Made in the USA
Charleston, SC
30 June 2013